UNLEASHED

Unlocking the Power of Corporate Prayer

By: Susan Rowe

Endorsements for *Unleashed*

Many excellent books have been written about prayer, but few focus on the necessity and the power of corporate prayer. In this book, my friends, Drs. Fred & Sue Rowe (co-founders of the Global Watch movement) along with various notable contributors unapologetically bring forth corporate prayer as not only a crucial praxis in the church, but a core identity of the Church (Ekklesia). The content of this book will give you courage especially during this time of unprecedented great shakings and birth pangs around the nations. It will also challenge you to take action, re-align your priorities and give yourself to meaningful watchfulness that will bear eternal fruits.

—DANIEL LIM,
Author, Bible 360
CEO, International House of Prayer Kansas City (2008-2020)

We see it happening before our very eyes. Everything that can be shaken is being shaken. This is the urgent moment for leaders within Christ's Church to have our spiritual eyes opened to see with clarity God's heavenly supply chain for the sustaining grace and overcoming victory these days require. We will not effectively lead our churches or move forward into our destiny by doing business as usual. These days demand our full embrace of the prayer model that Jesus Himself has given us. Jesus said, "My house shall be called a house of prayer for all nations." In "Unleashed," Dr. Susan Rowe helps us understand, in a very compelling way, how we the Church, can step into our finest hour.

Dr. Susan Rowe and her husband Dr. Frederic Rowe have faithfully and dynamically led the prayer ministry of Canyon Hills Church for over two decades. As their pastor, I have witnessed firsthand the resulting and remarkably supernatural favor of God that continues to this day.

—WENDELL VINSON
Pastor of Canyon Hills Church, Bakersfield, CA
Co-Founder and President of CityServe

Over the history of the church, many insightful books have been written on prayer, particularly from a devotional or theological point of view, less so from a functional or imperative view. In *Unleashed*, Susan Rowe sets the mission of prayer loose upon us all. Pulling those various strands into a beautiful tapestry, Rowe draws valuable synthesis and symmetry from those many insights into a glorious thunder of the privilege and power uniquely released in *corporate prayer*. Read this book, then find people, and pray together!

—DEAN BRIGGS
Author, *Ekklesia Rising*
IHOPKC Chief Strategist, VP Messaging
@dbarkleybriggs; deanbriggs.com

A concise, clear call to the great need and power of corporate prayer! Biblically sound, well documented, uniquely relevant, this book reawakens and realigns the church to take her place as the "House of Prayer" for all nations. A must-read for all pastors, leaders, and congregations in this critical hour!

—PASTOR GREG SIMAS
Founder, Convergence House of Prayer

Unleashed: Unlocking the Power of Corporate Prayer expresses the heart of the Father calling His Church back to a place of corporate prayer before His throne. Sue Rowe's timely research reveals how far we have drifted away from the power of such prayer in the early church, and how weakened we have become as a result.

We live in a time of great shaking, resulting in the rise and fall of nations and the increasing threat of nuclear war. Isaiah 60:1 describes a time of darkness over the earth and deep darkness over the people yet gives the promise that the Lord will arise and His glory seen. The Lord of hosts is releasing His end time instructions to His corporate prayer army, preparing for His glory to be revealed.

If you are one of His soldiers, then this book is for you. It will take you deeper, instructing and equipping you in a way you have not previously experienced.

—JENNY HAGGER

Director, Australian House of Prayer for All Nations

How powerful is corporate prayer? As Susan Rowe rightly mentions on the very first page of this timely and provocative book, corporate prayer birthed the New Testament Church—a Church so powerful that the gates of hell will never prevail against it. That's how powerful corporate prayer is!

In this book, Susan demonstrates how essential corporate prayer was for the early Church and how believers gathered regularly for the purpose of prayer (Acts 2:40-47). She describes how God responded to their prayers and worked mighty miracles in response to their consistent and fervent prayers. Corporate prayer was undeniably a foundational and key element of the early church.

The book also tells us about how corporate prayer sets a foundation for oneness and for unity. We know from Psalm 133 that unity pleases God and provokes Him to activate the anointing and command a blessing upon His people and the nations at large. Be encouraged to read about how corporate prayer unifies, edifies, strengthens and inspires the Body of Yeshua.

This book is sounding a trumpet call to the Body of Yeshua Hamashiach in love, to return to its original blueprint and mandate and become the "house of prayer for all nations" that it was ordained to be. We are reminded that we cannot fulfill the Great commission spoken of in Matthew 28:19 to disciple all nations, until we first become a house of prayer for all nations.

In my own personal life, corporate prayer has proven invaluable. As a new believer in January 1983 who did not know how to pray, I learned how to pray by going to corporate prayer gatherings and listening to the more mature believers pray. Corporate prayers discipled, strengthened and encouraged me to stand strong and remain in the faith.

May God continue to ignite corporate prayer in the prayer networks and movements, within the established Assemblies and in the nations overall! Thank you Lord for transformational revival that is being birthed in the nations and for using this book for Your glory to fan the sparks of revival!

—PEARL KUPE
Global Voice of Prayer (Africa)

Well-researched, written, footnoted and scholarly - yet heartfelt and warm - Dr. Susan Rowe's latest book, Unleashed, will stir readers to pray. With contributions from Dr. Fred Rowe, Unleashed highlights communities of prayer marked by love, fellowship, honor, passion, joy and faith. Written by the Rowes with contributions from pastors and global prayer leaders, *Unleashed* is a reminder of the value Jesus places on personal and communal prayer. Drawing from the rich, personal, devoted prayer lives of people now gathered around the throne of God, *Unleashed* provides well-documented, historical accounts of the prayer-fueled ministries of men and women who passionately pursued Jesus and contended for revival in their generations.

—STEVE REES
Freelance writer for Christian publications, and former news reporter

What a timely gift to the Body of Christ in this hour! In this book, Dr. Sue Rowe so poignantly reminds the Church of our history of being the faithful remnant in a generation to stand in the gap between the inevitability of what we are seeing and the possibilities not yet seen of what God can do when the Church prays. If we are to be ones who shift history in our day, we must embrace this prophetic message to become contending communities of prayer who will set our hearts to pray "in one accord" until we see the fullness of His promises in our generation.

Sue, thank you for faithfully calling the Church back to its true identity of being the joyful "house of prayer for all nations."

—THAI LAM

Executive Director, Luke 18 Project, IHOPKC and Collegiate Day of Prayer

As I have read through, and studied, *Unleashed*, I have found myself firmly rooted and grounded in the love of our Messiah. This book is truly a guide to raising up corporate prayer in these perilous times. I heartily endorse "Unleashed," and am praying that every believer will add this volume to his or her library.

—SARA BALLENGER

Capitol Hill Prayer Partners

Now, more than ever before, there is an urgent need for the power of corporate prayer to be restored and released through the Body of Messiah in Israel and the nations. Sue Rowe's deeply insightful and timely book, "Unleashed," gives great clarity to the principles behind this vital key for the advancing of the Kingdom of God in the face of growing end-time darkness. May this book be used by the Lord to impact multitudes of leaders and members of His body worldwide to re-ignite and mobilize corporate prayer in these challenging days ahead.

—KAREN DAVIS

Co-Founder/Worship Director
Kehilat HaCarmel, Mt. Carmel, Israel

UNLEASHED

Unlocking the Power of Corporate Prayer

BY: SUSAN ROWE

CONTRIBUTORS:

DR. FREDERIC ROWE: Co-Founder, The Global Watch

PASTOR SHELDON KIDWELL: Bay City Church, Cape Town, South Africa

PASTOR GREG SIMAS: Founder, Convergence House of Prayer, Fremont, CA

JENNY HAGGER: Founder, Australian House of Prayer for All Nations, Adelaide, Australia

KAREN DAVIS: Co-Founder/Worship Director, Kehilat Ha Carmel, Mt. Carmel, Israel

The Global Watch
PO Box 10972
5501 Stockdale Highway
Bakersfield, CA 93389

theglobalwatch.com

Published in the United States of America

ISBN: 9780578303888

DEDICATION

T o my husband Fred whose endless support, wisdom, and insight has supported me through the process of writing this book, I cannot thank you enough. As a man of peace, you have been a steady light and continued source of encouragement for not only me but our three sons and families to run the race set before us to finish the task.

And to the growing family and clusters of watchmen and worshippers faithfully gathering on the spiritual frontlines, may this book be a source of encouragement and strength to you on your "watch." May its message keep you steady in the days of battle and filled with times of rejoicing and steadfast in hope—and all the more as we see the Day approaching (Hebrews 10:25)!

Then the Lord answered me and said:
Write the vision
And make it plain on tablets,
That he may run who reads it.
Habakkuk 2:2

Contents

FOREWORD

I n our personal lives, prayer is the bedrock of our relational journeys with the Father, through the Son, and by the Spirit. Combining prayer with the living Word, this relationship grows. You learn to trust, know the heart of the Father, and see faith arise from the place of Sonship.

There is an invitation from the Lord to transition the Body of Christ from individual prayer security to corporate prayer expression. When we read the Gospels, we see how Jesus modeled this relationship with the Father for His disciples. In one example, He retreated to be with His Father in the Garden of Gethsemane. At this moment of deep despair and anguish, He asked Peter, James and John to come with him to watch and pray. There was an invitation for them to enter in, but they were not carrying the same burden as Jesus. Hence, the heavy eyes and the struggle to stay awake:

> "And He came to the disciples and found them sleeping. And He said to Peter, 'So, could you not watch with me one hour? Watch and pray that you may not enter into temptation. The Spirit indeed is willing, but the flesh is weak.'" Matthew 26:40-41

Later, when they faced the reality of needing to wait on the Lord in the Upper Room, when they suffered persecution and trial, or when they called on the name of the Lord while imprisoned, the disciples came alive in prayer. They were practicing what was modeled for them by Jesus, so that it became second nature by the empowerment of the Spirit.

Today, the Church has walked into a new era, and we believe new wine is being poured out. For it to be received, we need to allow our wineskins to be made ready. The new is not put into the old, but into that which is fresh and rejuvenated. This involves taking an old wineskin and soaking it in water until the leather becomes pliable and soft. Once the whole skin is ready, oil is rubbed into the hide to seal it.

This renewal is often the same spiritual process of rejuvenation that we go through to embrace change and receive our new wine. We allow the water of the Spirit to soak over the hard parts of our hearts formed from old mindsets, traditions, or practices. In this era, we are opening ourselves to embrace the new, and be positioned to become pliable receptors of this fresh move of God. Anointing oil is poured upon our hearts as a seal of equipping and empowering. This process can be painful, lonely and can take time. But, as we wait upon the Lord, He will "renew our strength; and we will mount up with wings like eagles, we will run and not grow weary, we will walk and not be faint" (Isaiah 40:31).

With the headwinds of challenging times before us, we are in a season of re-establishing the hidden power of corporate prayer. By rallying the Church, we embark on a journey of discovery and experience its transforming power. In taking up this challenge, we can say, as Paul the Apostle says in 2 Corinthians 5:16, "We regard no one according to the flesh" as a true community of the Spirit arises as one in prayer.

This book models the beauty of corporate prayer that does not look like the weekly prayer meeting attended by the few faithful few; rather it is a catalytic call for people to take their stand and position themselves to *watch and pray.* We trust you will glean from testimonies and the foundations laid within these pages to see the success of corporate prayer within your own community.

Sheldon Kidwell, Pastor, Bay City Church, Cape Town, South Africa

PREFACE

W hat communities of committed prayer accomplish are not well understood in the "numbers" driven Christian culture today. Yet, in these small cells are elements of covenant, agreement, relationship, and kingdom realities that shake heaven and earth. Those called to the house of prayer are now being more readily heard in a Church being increasingly challenged by the headwinds of turmoil, and moral decline. In the coming storm, these small cells may very well be the herald and lamppost for the awakening of the body of Christ that is increasingly being called to the frontline of battle. This book investigates the biblical foundations of corporate prayer, its character and nature, its challenges, relativity, revival history, and importance for today, but ultimately, its redemption and catalytic power to mobilize the Church into its finest hour.

ACKNOWLEDGEMENTS

I want to personally thank friends and family who have generated prayers and support throughout the research and efforts in this book. Your prayers and encouragement have been an invaluable source of love and example of God's faithfulness.

Thank you to the guidance and editing help from Gail Levin whose insights have helped me write the vision and "make it plain." Her editing skills you will enjoy throughout the book.

Thank you to Daniel Lim, who, despite a busy schedule, took time to read, lend insights and theological review. Thank you also to Dean Briggs and Greg Simas, who reviewed, contributed to, and supported this work from pastoral and apostolic perspectives. Also, I have learned so much from Karen Davis, a dear friend and beautiful worship leader whom I consider a mother in Israel, for her understanding from a Hebraic perspective. Her perceptions have sharpened me, and her faithfulness to stand in her call to Israel has blessed the nations.

Thank you to our local church body, and pastoral leadership at Canyon Hills Church. Your receptivity and faithfulness in prayer and service to our city is an example of a beacon of light amid darkness for all who attend and for the community. Your faithfulness in prayer has opened the door to serve the nation and the nation(s).

And to the beautiful family of Watchmen in the nations responding to the call to build community in prayer from local expressions to global connections, I send my deepest appreciation for your dedication, faith, and perseverance. Thank you to Sheldon Kidwell, Jenny Hagger for your friendship and example of authentic servant leadership. Your contributions and assistance were invaluable in the process of the formation of this book. Your friendship and insights have been a joyful strength to both Fred and I. God is preparing an Isaiah 62:6-7 people who will not relent, and who will stand to see His Kingdom come and will be done, on earth as it is in heaven!

Introduction and Definitions:

The purpose of this book is to inspire and re-ignite the call for corporate prayer. In years of serving the local church body and the wider prayer movement, it became increasingly evident that corporate prayer, as a central practice of today's church, is quite different today than what was expressed in the book of Acts. Though many books and research have been done examining individual prayer experience, few have investigated the corporate prayer expression. In these troubled times, the purpose of this book is to re-expose the need for and re-ignite the biblical foundations for the church to be a "house of prayer for all nations."

In reading this book, it will be important to understand some of the terms. Below are a few definitions that will help lend insight as you read:

Corporate Prayer: Defined biblically as, "Wherever two or more are gathered in His name," Matthew 18:20. An acronym is a contending community of prayer. Worship is an integral part of corporate prayer expression. When two or more are gathered together, it is synonymous with the term *prayer watch.*

Ekklesia or Church: A gathering of citizens called out from their homes into some public place for the purpose of deliberating.[1] That can be a local church or many churches gathering together. In the New Testament context, it would be a community of believers committed to contending prayer and relationship.

Prayer Watch: Community of contending prayer with intentional focus on God, the promises of His Word as it relates to the spiritual horizon.

church (small c): Webster's definition: "a building for the public especially for Christian worship."[2]

Prayer: Personal intimacy and deliberate, and unmediated communication with God. It involves our communication and relationship with God in prayer **and** worship. Troeger states that prayer, "Represents a living relationship with God"[3]

Cultural factor: "An ingredient within the traditions and rules of behavior held by a defined group that contributes greatly to a particular result or situation.[4]"

Prayer Movement: "A movement spanning denominations focusing on the pursuit of God as the focus of one's life. A Christian movement is a theological, political, or philosophical interpretation of Christianity that is not generally represented by a specific church, sect, or denomination.[5]" This definition is a collective term applying to houses of prayer, prayer ministries, or prayer groups that abound both inside and outside the formal Church walls.

House of Prayer: A house of prayer carries a functional identity as a place where the primary focus is on prayer and worship in community. The International House of Prayer in Kansas City has adopted this definition:

> "The Lord has called us to be a community of believers committed to God, each other, and to establishing and maintaining a 24/7 house of prayer in Kansas City—a perpetual solemn assembly gathering corporately to fast and pray in the spirit of the tabernacle of David."[6]

Many houses of prayer in the nations use the term, "In the spirit of the tabernacle of David," as part of their defining vision. This definition primarily refers to the primacy of both worship and prayer exalting God through music, declarations of the written Word, and prayer. The importance for the Church is to realize the call to establish and perpetuate the House of Prayer is not only through Isaiah's and Jesus' words, but also as relayed in 1 Peter 2:9-10:

> *But you are a chosen generation, a royal priesthood, a holy nation, His own special people, that you may proclaim the praises of Him who called you out of darkness into His marvelous light; who once were not a people but are now the people of God, who had not obtained mercy but now have obtained mercy.*

1

THE RECALL: BIBLICAL FOUNDATIONS FOR THE HOUSE OF PRAYER

It is written, My house shall be called
a house of prayer for all nations
Mark 11:17

Today, as trials, disasters, wars, rumors of war, and tribulations form the headlines of newsrooms, the Church and its role in our lives and corporate body are being tested. COVID-19, lawlessness and natural disasters have erupted across the nations testing the heartbeat of the Church. Many Christians are witnessing laws being issued pressuring them to conform to standards that violate their biblical values. The plethora of reforms emanating from legislation impacting education and social standards are endangering the moral fabric of future generations. With the challenges of the times, the Church is being thrust into a virtual crisis of identity. What is the *foundational* identity of the Church? Amid the storms, what is God saying to the Body of Christ? How do we respond to the challenges today?

As COVID-19 hit the nations, a dynamic shift commenced, impacting all cultural spheres of influence. The usual rhythm of life, worship, and relating changed. God has used the pandemic to draw the church out of its customary four walls. It is doubtful that we will go back

Church of God. As God's house is a house where the business of praying is carried on, so is it a place where the business of making praying people out of prayerless people is done. The house of God is a Divine workshop, and there the work of prayer goes on. Or the house of God is a Divine schoolhouse, in which the lesson of prayer is taught; where men and women learn to pray, and where they are graduated, in the school of prayer. Any church calling itself the house of God, and failing to magnify prayer; which does not put prayer in the forefront of its activities; which does not teach the great lesson of prayer, should change its teaching to conform to the Divine pattern or change the name of its building to something other than a house of prayer."[4]

Luke records a particularly poignant moment when Jesus drew near to Jerusalem for the last time. He stopped and wept. Why? Was it for the pain and persecution He was about to endure? No! Luke records Jesus' words:

> *"If you had known even you, especially in this your day, the things that make for your peace. But now they are hidden from your eyes. For days will come upon you when your enemies will build an embankment around you, surround you and close you in on every side, and level you, and your children within you, to the ground; and they will not leave in you one stone upon another, because you did not know the time of your visitation"* (Luke 19:41-44).

His tears were for the welfare of a city that could not recognize what God was doing. Perhaps Jesus' heart was pondering what would happen a few decades later when Jerusalem would be leveled by Roman invaders in 70 AD. His eyes may also have been seeing the future and the end-time narrative spoken of by the prophets where enemies from the nations would invade and utterly try to destroy Israel. Either scenario would fit the description relayed by Luke. The bottom line:

Jesus was concerned that people were distracted and turned away from God, and an earth-shattering, tectonic event was about to occur.

What happened next? Jesus went to the temple. Given the concern He had just experienced and expressed, His eyes beheld the moneychangers in the temple engrossed in their daily bartering and trading. Jesus' bold entry unleashed His passionate love for His House. Dismayed by the money changers, He reminded those selling goods of Isaiah's prophecy, *"It is written, My house shall be called a house of prayer"* (Isaiah 56:7, Matthew 21:13, Mark 11:17, Luke 19:46).

To emphasize His point, Jesus then assertedly turned the tables over, reminding all present that "His house," the temple, is to be a house of prayer, a gathering place for prayer and worship of God; not a "den of thieves" (Matthew 21:13, Mark 11:17, Luke 19:46). One can only imagine the concern Jesus had for the condition of His house. By His own declarations and actions that day, Jesus came to earth, in part, to establish the priestly identity of the Church as a "house of prayer for all nations." Cleansing the temple was an act of clearing the deck of the distractions so that people could see and hear Him. Matthew records what happened next, *Then the blind and the lame came to Him in the temple, and He healed them* (Matthew 21:14). Luke further notes, *And He was teaching daily in the temple...for all the people were very attentive to hear Him* (Luke 19:47-48).

OVERVIEW OF THE TIMES:

Today, it may not be overt money changers in the House of the Lord, but in reality, can we say that what we are experiencing is a "house of prayer" in our local congregations? Are we functioning as "a chosen generation, a royal priesthood, a holy nation" that Peter speaks of in 1 Peter 2:9? Dr. James Banks, noted church planter and pastor, writes, "There is no greater need in the church today than for Christians to recapture the lost art of praying together."[5] P.J. Johnson corroborates with this view saying, "Prayer unites puny man to Almighty God in miraculous partnership. It is the most noble and most essential ministry God gives to His children-but is the most neglected."[6] As crises escalate, the need to understand and recapture this time-honored power engine of the Church will be vital. The world is rapidly changing, with end-time narratives playing out before us. No matter what your eschatology is, one cannot deny that times are intensifying.

A harbinger of the season we are now in exploded onto the global scene with the attack on the World Trade Center in New York City and Pentagon in Washington DC on September 11, 2001. It was a birth pang, a cataclysmic event that changed perspectives in travel, religion, government and international relations, to name a few. Initially, corporate prayer mobilized across the nation as people gathered to pray. I was called to help mobilize prayer during the painful weeks following the attacks. However, the passionate prayers that followed the attacks largely dissipated a few short months later. Responses of people to pray in the corporate environment faded away.

As the dampened response became evident, a study by Barna Research Group in December 2001 articulated the concern, "After the 9-11 attacks, religious activity surged, but within two months, virtually every spiritual indicator available suggested that things were back to pre-attack levels."[7] Later, in 2006, Barna followed up with research on the lasting influence of 9/11 on America's faith. The study noted, "Despite an intense surge in religious activity and expression in the weeks immediately following 9/11, the faith of Americans is virtually indistinguishable today compared to pre-attack conditions."[8]

How did we miss this wake-up call to America and furthermore into the nations? James Banks offers an explanation:

> "It may be no coincidence that the culture we live in has become increasingly indifferent and even hostile to Christianity at the same time that united prayer has gone out of the church. As recently as fifty years ago, prayer meetings were a vital part of many churches. As American culture became increasingly entertainment oriented, the mid-week prayer meeting was replaced by the Wednesday night service.

—

> The active work of prayer was replaced with passive listening as the focal point shifted from God's power to answer prayer to what was happening at the front of the church. Eventually, the prayer meeting moved out of the sanctuary and into a corner of the church library. At the same time, the church's impact upon culture around us began to decline."[9]

In addition, having worked in prayer ministry, it is my observation the evangelical church does not widely practice corporate prayer. Calling people to join in corporate prayer sessions is a challenge. John Spina notes, "To say that the typical American church does not pray together effectively and regularly does not seem to be an understatement."[10] Howard Lawler, pastor and author, states, "The label 'corporate prayer' reasonably applies to prayer shared by the larger body. Most American evangelical churches lack that experience."[11]

These assertions are reflected in recent studies. Ridgeway noted that though many people pray individually, "Less than 5% pray in corporate settings."[12] In 2017, Barna Research found only, "2% of Americans pray audibly or collectively with a church."[13] The title of the article articulates the research, "Silent and Solo: How Americans Pray."

If the attacks of 9/11 did not wake up the church to gather and pray, what would it take? If such an attack could raise only a passing interest, what would need to happen to have corporate prayer become a part of our normal Christian walk and not just a reactionary response to events? Experiencing this cataclysmic event and seeing the deterioration and lack of response from the Church has been a quest that God has highlighted over the ensuing years and is, in part, a catalyst for this book.

Today, it must be noted that God is igniting corporate prayer. However, much of it occurs outside the established church in the plethora of prayer ministries, houses of prayer, home groups, etc. Movements identified through lists of 24/7 houses of prayer in Europe and elsewhere continue to crop up. We will discuss more of this in chapter 6. Additionally, in the headwinds of the COVID 19 pandemic, interest in prayer has escalated. Jeanet Bentzen found in her report May,

2020, that daily data searches for prayer on Google reached the highest level ever recorded. The rise amounted to 50% of previous levels for prayer searches.[14] People do turn to God when in distress. Biblically, God often uses adversity to wake-up His people. Peter exhorts:

> *In this you greatly rejoice, though now for a little while, if need be, you have been grieved by various trials, that the genuineness of your faith, being much more precious than gold that perishes, though it is tested by fire, may be found to praise, honor, and glory at the revelation of Jesus Christ* (1 Peter 1:6-7).

We are in challenging times in which we will be tested. God uses challenges to strengthen us. The New Testament Church was birthed in a hostile and resistant Roman culture and rule. Now today, through this epidemic, God is testing the heartbeat of His Church. Will it respond and turn to the "One Thing" of which the psalmist speaks in Psalm 27:4, *One thing I have desired of the Lord, that will I seek; that I may dwell in the house of the Lord all the days of my life, to behold the beauty of the Lord and to inquire in His temple.* The lasting influence of COVID 19 catalyzing intensified prayer remains to be seen.

We are now in the times that Jesus spoke of in Matthew 24:24 when deception is skyrocketing, and Christian values are increasingly put on the chopping block of social and political opinion. Given the results of these studies and observations, we are looking at the looming possibility of the great falling away of which Paul warns: *Let no one deceive you by any means; for that Day will not come unless the falling away comes first, and the man of sin is revealed* (2 Thessalonians 2:3). To meet this deception is a relatively prayerless Church caught in the crossfires of a heavenly war of which it knows little. There will be a need to recover the centrality of corporate prayer in the church today to catapult it into the power expressed in Acts to heal, deliver and herald in the end-time harvest. None of this is written to criticize, but rather to lend clarity and understanding to help direct us to rediscover and re-evaluate how to resurrect this time-honored ministry today.

—

What needs to be cleaned up and re-arranged to see the priority of prayer, particularly corporate prayer, as the centerpiece of the church culture again? We will explore that question throughout this book in hopes that eyes will open and hearts receive His call.

REVIEWING BIBLICAL FOUNDATIONS:

In contrast, the expression of prayer was almost entirely corporate in reviewing the book of Acts. Corporate prayer carries a rich biblical history as a vital practice for God's people. In particular, the first Christians, as portrayed in the book of Acts, were a praying community. From Jesus and His twelve disciples to the one-hundred twenty in the Upper Room, community in prayer was an active part of the early Church culture and a catalyst to its growth. As a result, Christianity exploded on the face of the earth. The foundations laid by the Apostles and Prophets were birthed in the corporate prayer experience. Luke describes the community life of the first believers:

> *And they continued steadfastly in the apostles' doctrine and fellowship, in the breaking of bread, and in prayers. Then fear came upon every soul, and many wonders and signs were done through the apostles...So continuing daily with one accord in the temple, and breaking bread from house to house, they ate their food with gladness and simplicity of heart, praising God and having favor with all the people. And the Lord added to the church daily those who were being saved* (Acts 2:42-43;46-47).

These Scriptures portray the early Church as a dedicated praying community. All but one prayer setting recorded in Acts involved a corporate environment. The one exception is in Acts 10. Cornelius relays a personal encounter in prayer; however, that encounter led to a significant door to the Gospel opening for the Gentiles. All other mentions of prayer/worship involved at least two people in the prayer

---

setting. At Pentecost, believers were together in "one accord." Through Luke's careful documentation of the life of the early Church, numerous times, he relays the prominent role of day-to-day corporate prayer in the lives of Jesus' followers. Early Christian life was infused with the power that emanated from this time-honored practice. John Whitsett states in his research on corporate prayer:

> "The early followers of Jesus routinely turned to corporate prayer and utilized it as a source of power and means of breakthrough when faced with overwhelming circumstances. They considered corporate prayer an essential element of the meaning of being a part of his body. From all evidence it was woven into the fabric of their lives and regarded as an indispensable component of how their faith was expressed."[15]

Dr. Olusoga Akintunde's research also corroborates, "The apostles and the early Church had cultural issues but they thrived physically, numerically and spiritually due to the unwavering commitments to a culture of persistent, faithful and a community-based approach to prayer (Acts 6:4; Ephesians 1:16-23; 3:14-20; Colossians 1:9-27; and Philippians 4: 6-7)."[16]

Furthermore, prayers propelled the activity of the Holy Spirit throughout the book of Acts. Sixteen of the twenty-eight chapters mention the Holy Spirit. Other chapters documented the work of the Holy Spirit moving in the works of the apostles and early Church. God's supernatural interventions are recorded throughout the book. Stott explains the power of the Holy Spirit in the early Church: "One thing is certain. Christ's church had been overwhelmed by the Holy Spirit, who thrust it out to witness."[17]

Jesus set the example with His disciples by frequently drawing them together to pray. Gathering regularly, whether in public places, private homes, out in nature, they often joined as a community in prayer. Banks notes, "For the first three hundred years of Church history, the early Church had no formal buildings, no personal Bibles, no multi-media, and no sound systems. But they prayed persistently, and God moved in amazing ways as a result."[18] In fact, in His book, *And the Place Was Shaken*, John Franklin reviewed Jesus' use of the word "you" while teaching on prayer. He found thirty-seven verses. "You" was plural in thirty-three of the verses, and either plural or singular in four.[19] Corporate prayer was undoubtedly a natural part of the first Church and a vital part of the community of believers. In a resistant and challenging culture, corporate prayer was a unifying and catalytic force for the early Church and its exponential growth.

Jesus spoke of the power of Christian unity, *"That they all may be one, as You, Father, are in Me, and I in You; that they also may be one in Us, that the world may believe that You sent Me"* (John 17:21). This unity is a witness to the world that God sent Jesus. Ben Patterson writes, "The greatest argument for the authority and identity of Jesus comes not only from theologians and apologists. It can come from the simplest believers who will live together in the unity of the Holy Spirit!"[20] George Buttrick reiterates this foundation by noting, "The Christian enterprise began not in an organization, but in the group prayer of Jesus and His disciples."[21]

SUMMARY:

It can be safely extracted that corporate prayer was a foundational characteristic of the early Church. The temple was a place of corporate worship, at least for some time in the early life of the Church. Homes were a gathering place for smaller groups to fellowship and pray. Both played a vital role in fostering a culture of prayer. Stott remarks:

> "In his Gospel he (Luke) says 'they stayed continually at the temple, praising God,' Luke 24:53, and in the Acts that in the room where they were lodging, 'they all joined together constantly in prayer in the home.' It was a healthy combination: continuous praise in the temple, and continuous prayer in the home."[22]

Prayer was a priority, particularly the corporate expression. It fueled the actions of believers, led to miracles, and empowered a bold stance in the face of opposition. The prophetic message of Isaiah 56:7, His house is to be a "house of prayer for all nations," became a reality in the early Church.

The question then is raised, what has happened to the role of corporate prayer in the Church today? Briggs relays:

> "Church culture has a wonderful mix of pastoral, teaching and communal functions, but the necessary future begs for a church that will expand its identity and mission with *ekklesial*, territorial thinking. When we realize we are the *ekklesia*, a "prayerdigm shift" is inevitable because the word itself properly aligns our identity with government and prayer as Jesus intended."[23]

Review of the literature, and research on corporate prayer and its nature conveys the message reflected in the reality of its role in the Body of Christ today. Taking a close look at the character and nature of prayer in the Bible is not an uncommon focus of attention. Many books have been written on prayer that are powerful and effective. However, much of the literature and research is by and large about individual prayer. It is important to have our individual relationship with God honed and crafted in our personal journeys. Lawler states it well, "I write as one who took too long to become "woke" to corporate prayer. I don't mind disturbing the similar slumber of others so they can thrive. Corporate prayer is no 'weak and idle theme.' It is a vital theme. We are weak, but God is strong. We are shadows, but Jesus is sovereign. If we pray well in His name, we will fare well indeed."[24] In these troubled times, God is now beginning to open eyes to the primacy—scripturally and historically—of establishing community in prayer/worship.

The purpose of this book is to investigate corporate prayer in the body of Christ to fuel the fire Malachi describes, "*For from the rising of the sun, even to its going down, My name shall be great among the Gentiles; In every place incense shall be offered to My name, and a pure offering; for My name shall be great among the nations,*" *says the Lord of hosts* (Malachi 1:11). We will investigate the biblical foundations of corporate prayer, its character and nature, its challenges, relativity and importance for today, but ultimately, its redemption and catalytic power to mobilize God's Church into its finest hour.

DISCUSSION QUESTIONS:

1. In reviewing the chapter, what in your mind would the Acts 2:42-43, 46-47 church look like in your church or neighborhood?
2. How would you describe "A House of Prayer," based on Isaiah 56:7 and Matthew 21:13 in your own words?
3. Discuss the role of every Christ follower that is implied in "A House of Prayer for All nations." What things can you do to build up or start a local corporate prayer expression?
4. What barriers keep you from contributing to corporate prayer and how can you overcome them?

PRAYER POINTS:

1. Identify and pray for barriers to be broken down that prevent a greater fellowship and corporate prayer expression in your local church/congregation.
2. Pray for church leaders to receive and be encouraged through corporate prayer.

ACTION STEPS:

1. Take steps to develop your personal prayer life, i.e. committing to a daily discipline.
2. If you have a passion for prayer, open discussions with your church leadership on how to help "Unleash" your local church corporate prayer expression.

2

THE REVIEW: THE CHARACTER AND NATURE OF CORPORATE PRAYER IN THE EARLY CHURCH AND THE BOOK OF ACTS

And they continued steadfastly in the apostles' doctrine
and fellowship, in the breaking of bread, and in prayers.
Acts 2:42

While conveying the importance of corporate prayer, I have often said the prayers of a righteous man avail much (James 5:16); but corporate prayer changes history. How can I say that and substantiate it as true? We will explore this question in this chapter and attempt to relay the conviction in enough detail to inspire people to pursue it.

The most compelling role of corporate prayer in history comes from the book of Acts. It's pages tell the story of how the early Christians walked out their faith, were vigilant in prayer, and overcame a hostile environment to spread the Gospel. Stott notes, "We are given four accounts of Jesus, but only one of the early Church. So, the Acts occupies an indispensable place in the Bible."[1]

Corporate prayer was an integral part of the first Christian's journey in faith. As mentioned earlier, all but one prayer setting recorded in Acts involved a corporate environment. All others involved at least two people. Through Luke's careful documentation of the life of the early believers, numerous times he relays the prominent role of day-to-day corporate prayer in the life of Jesus' followers.

Akintunde affirms, "The apostles and the early Church had cultural issues, but they thrived physically, numerically and spiritually due to the unwavering commitments to a culture of persistent, faithful and a community-based approach to prayer (Acts 6:4; Ephesians 1: 16-23; 3: 14-20; Colossians 1: 9-27; and Philippians 4: 6-7)."[2]

In studying corporate prayer in the Book of Acts, John Spina writes, "What I found was that in writing Acts, Luke was far more interested in showing the attitudes and characteristics of the people in the early Church and that these were reflected in the practice and discipline of corporate prayer."[3]   D. Edmond Hiebert notes, "If the Church today would regain the spiritual power of the early Church it must recover the truth and practice of prayer as a vital working force."[4]   What was it the first believers experienced and understood that fueled a desire to follow Jesus with passion and vigor?

While reading this chapter, please keep in mind the context in which the Scriptures were written. Corporate prayer conveyed in Acts was a central praxis to their community. When expressed today, **it is fun!** The expression is not confined to the obscure group backstage or church library quietly praying. When implemented, it is a dynamic force for the advance of His Kingdom and can inspire relational strength and spiritual fervency to all involved.

To review the characteristics of the early Church, we will look at seven notable virtues of corporate prayer woven throughout the book of Acts. The attributes described all have to do with the nature and culture of their communities in prayer. Though not exclusive, these seven qualities express distinct themes that flow throughout the narrative to characterize corporate prayer. The Scriptures used are not meant to be exhaustive, but rather qualitative attributes of the prayer life of the early Church.

1. BEING TEACHABLE AND PATIENT:

Acts 1:4,7-8: *And being assembled together with them, He commanded them not to depart from Jerusalem, but to wait for the Promise of the Father which, He said, "You have heard from Me; for John truly baptized with water, but you shall be baptized with the Holy Spirit not many days from now," v.4...And He said to them, "It is not for you to know times or seasons which the Father has put in His own authority. But you shall receive power when the Holy Spirit has come upon you; and you shall be witnesses to Me in Jerusalem, and in all Judea and Samaria, and to the end of the earth" v. 7-8.* (Also in Acts 2:44; 4:32-34)

As the book of Acts opens, the believers were *assembled together* (Acts 1:4). Jesus suddenly appeared to them and promised, *"But you shall be baptized with the Holy Spirit not many days from now,"* (Acts 1:5). The word *baptized* or *βαπτίζω baptizō* means being fully immersed. In other words, Jesus assured those gathered they would be completely immersed in the Holy Spirit in a few days. Through this empowerment, the Gospel would spread and the Church would grow. Jesus did not speak to them individually but corporately, preparing them for the outpouring of His Spirit.

Such a promise immediately stirred eager questions amongst those gathered. *"Lord, will You at this time restore the kingdom to Israel?"* (Acts 1:6). Jesus' answer heightened their quest but redirected their attention to waiting on the Father: *"It is not for you to know times or seasons which the Father has put in His own authority"* (Acts 1:7). His response shifted their focus by drawing their attention to the importance of the Holy Spirit for the future spread of the Gospel. In his commentary on Acts 1:8, John Stott describes the scope of the early Church's reach:

> "Chapters 1–7 describe events in Jerusalem, chapter 8 mentions the scattering of the disciples 'throughout Judea and Samaria' (8:1), and goes on to record the evangelization of a Samaritan city by Philip (8:5–24) and of 'many Samaritan villages' by the apostles Peter and John (8:25), while the

conversion of Saul in chapter 9 leads on in the rest of the book to his missionary expeditions, and finally to his journey to Rome."[5]

John Polhill, in his Bible commentary, describes this early spread of the Gospel: "The geographical scope of Acts 1:8 provides a rough outline of the entire book: Jerusalem (1–7), Judea and Samaria (8–12), the ends of the earth (13–28)."[6] Characteristics of teachability and openness in the believers manifested by willingness to wait for the Holy Spirit. Through this simple act of waiting, the Church would experience a supernatural power that unleashed the Gospel to the nations.

This moment was a critical juncture in preparing believers for the Lord's final departure and subsequent empowerment through the gift of the Holy Spirit. The teachable attitude was evident amongst the corporate body of believers and set the stage for ongoing future communication with Jesus in prayer.

Willingly, they waited and received Jesus' words for what was to come, *"You shall be witnesses to Me in Jerusalem, and in all Judea and Samaria, and to the end of the earth"* (Acts 1:8). Without abiding and getting their directions from God, their spiritual lives would have been cut short or aborted. By their obedience in following Jesus' words, what could have been done in the flesh was multiplied exponentially. So also, today, the simplicity of "the wait" with a trusting obedient heart is the well-spring of empowerment that takes our feeble desires and re-works them into God's Divine plan. In other words—the wait is worth it!

2. PERSEVERING PRAYER:

Acts 1:12-14: *They returned to Jerusalem from the mount called Olivet, which is near Jerusalem, a Sabbath day's journey. And when they had entered, they went up into the upper room where they were staying: Peter, James, John, and Andrew; Philip and Thomas; Bartholomew and Matthew; James the son of Alphaeus and Simon the Zealot; and Judas the son of James. These all **continued with one accord in prayer and***

supplication, with the women and Mary the mother of Jesus, and with His brothers. (Acts 2:1, 42, 46; 4:24, 31; 5:12; 7:57; 8:6; 12:5)

Two characteristics describe the prayer-life of the early Church in this passage. They *continued;* in other words, they persevered, and they were in *one accord*, agreement.

The Greek word for *continued* according to Strong's concordance is, "προσκαρτερέω *proskartereō*; from roots 4314 and 2594; "to be earnest towards, i.e. (to a thing) to persevere, be constantly diligent, or (in a place) to attend assiduously all the exercises, or (to a person)."[7] Luke describes this vigilant attitude throughout Acts, (1:14, 2:42, 46; 6:4; 10:7).

In other words, community in prayer was not just an option; it was very much a central priority in their lives. Stott explains *continue* as, "God's promises do not render prayer superfluous. On the contrary, it is only His promises which give us the warrant to pray and the confidence that He will hear and answer."[8] Prayer was a priority in early Church leadership. Luke describes the leadership, *But we will give ourselves continually to prayer and to the ministry of the word* (Acts 6:4). As a result, persevering prayer was a constant characteristic in the lives of the first believers and rendered them effective in penetrating the resistant culture.

Living in a hostile culture, not only did they continue prayer in community, but they were of *one accord*. Stott further explains the nature of *one accord* as, "Both united prayer (Acts 4:24) and a united decision (Acts 15:25), so that the 'togetherness' implied seems to go beyond mere assembly and activity to agreement about what they were praying for."[9] We will investigate the further ramifications of prayer in one accord in the next chapter. Suffice it to say, commitment and agreement in prayer and community were the explosive dynamics that launched the first Church into a life-changing force on the earth.

For Christians to impact an ever challenging and resistant culture, this corporate, persevering prayer model needs to be raised up as central to the life of believers. When corporate prayer becomes an option, it is optional, and the centrality of its importance is lost in a flurry of activity.

It becomes one of the lowest attended meetings in the church. As a priority and central driving force for the Church—prayer will unleash the threshing instrument for an end-time harvest. Coming full circle to its original call, persevering corporate prayer carries the key to unlock the treasure trove of heaven's resources into a world desperately in need. No one leaves active corporate prayer sessions the same as the Spirit moves amongst people.

3. ACTIVATION OF BELIEVERS THROUGH SPIRITUAL RECOGNITION AND IMPARTATION:

Acts 1:24-26: *And they prayed and said, "You, O Lord, who know the hearts of all, show which of these two You have chosen to take part in this ministry and apostleship from which Judas by transgression fell, that he might go to his own place." And they cast their lots, and the lot fell on Matthias. And he was numbered with the eleven apostles.* (Also Acts 6:6; 8:17; 13:3; 14:23; 15:40; 19:6; 24:23; 28:8)

A corporate prayer dynamic of the first Church was the ability to identify and acknowledge leadership and the gifts amongst themselves that could be used to empower the first Christians. Casting lots was a way of identification. Stott notes casting lots was "a method of discerning God's will which was sanctioned in the Old Testament (Leviticus 16:8; Numbers 26:55, Proverbs 16:33), but which does not appear to have been used after the Spirit had come."[10] After the Holy Spirit, the laying on of hands was one of the powerful affirmations practiced. As a result, the early Church multiplied and expanded. In his commentary, John Polhill describes laying on of hands as follows:

> "In the Old Testament the laying on of hands deals with the transfer of some personal characteristic or responsibility from one person to another, as from Moses to Joshua, Num 27:16-23. The gesture is used in several ways in Acts: in healings, 9:17, the gift of the Spirit (9:17, 8:18), and in commissioning to a task (6:6; 13:3). Even in commissionings, the emphasis

---

19

is not so much an appointment to an office as to designation
for a task."[11]

By recognizing God-given abilities in others, the leaders practiced
the laying on of hands and commissioning people into their gifts and
callings. Such recognition in the body resulted in a two-fold dynamic:
First, believers were publicly recognized, empowered, and set into their
identities, gifts, and callings. Secondly, those in leadership were
relieved of much work and were able to focus on prayer. Luke describes
this powerful effect in Acts 6:3-7:

> *"Therefore, brethren, seek out from among you seven men of*
> *good reputation, full of the Holy Spirit and wisdom, whom we*
> *may appoint over this business; but we will give ourselves*
> *continually to prayer and to the ministry of the Word." And*
> *the saying pleased the whole multitude. And they chose*
> *Stephen, a man full of faith and the Holy Spirit, and Philip,*
> *Prochorus, Nicanor, Timon, Parmenas, and Nicolas, a*
> *proselyte from Antioch, whom they set before the apostles;*
> *and when they had prayed, they laid hands on them. Then the*
> *word of God spread, and the number of the disciples*
> *multiplied greatly in Jerusalem, and a great many of the*
> *priests were obedient to the faith.*

This pattern of identifying leadership through prayer and
acknowledging them publicly through the laying on of hands became an
essential tool for spreading the Gospel. In this instance, men were
chosen to oversee food distribution. The practice caused those chosen
to be recognized and empowered to do what they had been called to do.

Throughout Acts, the early Church continued to practice the laying
on of hands. Acts 13:2-3 relays such a corporate recognition, *As they
ministered to the Lord and fasted, the Holy Spirit said, "Now separate
to Me Barnabas and Saul for the work to which I have called them."
Then, having fasted and prayed, and laid hands on them, they sent them
away.* This practice is mentioned six times in Acts. As a result of this

continued intentional activity of recognizing gifts, Luke reflects, *So when they had appointed elders in every church, and prayed with fasting, they commended them to the Lord in whom they had believed* (Acts 14:23). The result was the spread of the Gospel through the multiplication of laborers. The leaders could then devote themselves to prayer and keep it a central dynamic in the community.

4. HOSPITALITY:

Acts 2:42: *And they continued steadfastly in the apostles' doctrine and fellowship, in the breaking of bread, and in prayers.* (Also Acts 9:43-10:48; 16:33-34)

Acts 2:42 relays the qualities of the early Church. Stott identifies four characteristics: "First, they were a learning church devoted to learning the apostles' teaching; second, they were loving and community-oriented in fellowship and breaking of bread; third, they were a worshipping praying church; and fourth, an evangelistic church.[12]" These words define a culture of hospitality that supported and propagated a contending community of prayer and effective evangelism. The nature of hospitality in Acts was a crucial catalyst in attracting and discipling new believers in the Church. *Fellowship*, or *koinonia* as mentioned in Acts 2:42, is descriptive. Polhill explains, "The Greek word used here (*koinōnia*) is one Paul often employed, but it appears only here in all of Luke-Acts...The meaning would then be that they devoted themselves to a fellowship that was expressed in their mutual meals and in their prayer life together."[13] The picture is of a church engaged with community and prayer. Luke further describes:

> *So, continuing daily with one accord in the temple, and breaking bread from house to house, they ate their food with gladness and simplicity of heart. Praising God and having favor with all the people. And the Lord added to the church daily those who were being saved (Acts 2:46-47).*

21

It must be noted that hospitality was a key characteristic nurturing the prayer life of the early Church.

Additionally, much of Jesus' ministry occurred in homes or outside in nature, sitting with the disciples and the crowds. He loved going to Mary and Martha's residence, and healed her brother, Lazarus, John 11:5, 17-27. He ministered by the Sea of Galilee, Luke 5:1; fed the five thousand, Matthew 14:13-21; and healed many who touched the hem of His garment in these hospitable environments, Matthew 15:34-36.

Later, in Philippi, Paul went to the riverside where "prayer was customarily made; and we sat down and spoke to the women who met there" (Acts 16:13). They met Lydia who "opened her heart to heed the things spoken by Paul and was baptized" (Acts 16:14). She invited them into her home to stay.

However, meeting resistance while in Philippi, Paul and Silas were beaten and imprisoned, Acts 16:16-24. Though brutalized and chained, Paul and Silas prayed and sang hymns. A great earthquake shook them free. In the tumult, the keeper of the prison feared for his life. He was about to draw his sword upon himself when Paul intervened, *"Do yourself no harm, for we are all here"* (Acts 16:28). The encounter led to the jailer inviting them into his home, wounds tended and cared for, and the jailer's entire family saved. *And he (the jailer) took them the same hour of the night and washed their stripes. And immediately he and all his family were baptized* (Acts 16:33). This kind of hospitality was a conduit of God's love, salvation and discipleship for new believers.

Today, hospitality continues to be a unique and God-given key that unlocks hearts to receive Christ. Hospitality opens the door for people to experience God's love. Jesus was a living example of ministering countless times in small intimate environments. We know ministries that simply bring food to pornography studios, the military, and those locked in prisons of drugs and despair. The door to relationship then opens. Hospitality invites the life-giving force of God's love and Presence into the midst of any gathering.

On one memorable evening, we had some youth over for a simple time of food and fellowship. Food set the course. It put everyone in a positive attitude making conversation easy. Worship and prayer naturally followed. At the end, one young man confessed he had been contemplating suicide before coming. Experiencing the love of Jesus amongst the people present broke the assignment. The rejection that haunted him was released, and he experienced adoption as a son through the beauty and simplicity of hospitality.

5. FAITH-FILLED PRAYERS THAT RELEASE HEALING AND EVANGELISM:

Acts 3:1-3: *Now Peter and John went up together to the temple at the hour of prayer, the ninth hour.* (Also in Acts 5:12-16; 6:3-4; 8:4-8; 9:17-19, 32-35, 40; 14:8-10, 19-23; 16:16-18, 25; 19:11-20; 20:7-16; 28:1-9)

Prayer was part of the intimate community culture of the Acts Church and directed their activity. As leaders, the disciples prioritized prayer. Shortly after Pentecost, Luke notes that Peter and John intentionally went to the temple at the ninth hour for the evening sacrifice. Matthew Henry, in his commentary, explains, "The ninth hour, that is, three o'clock in the afternoon, was one of the hours of prayer among the Jews."[14] Their diligence to pursue prayer and walk to the temple is notable. Polhill explains this hour further:

> "It was also the time of the evening *Tamid*, one of the two sacrifices held daily in the temple. These had become prescribed times of prayer, and people would come to the temple at the sacrifice times to observe the ceremony and pray. The largest crowds would thus have been found at the times of sacrifice, as Peter and John must have been well aware; for they went to the temple for prayer and for witness."[15]

By going to the Temple at this prescribed time of prayer, Peter and John reflected the discipline and intentionality in which they viewed and practiced prayer.

This diligence put them in a ready position, so that when they encountered a cripple, the Holy Spirit moved them to reach out and command healing: *Then Peter said, "Silver and gold I do not have, but what I do have I give you: In the name of Jesus Christ of Nazareth, rise up and walk"* (Acts 3:6). The man rose up and walked. Everyone present saw the healing power of Jesus manifest. As a result, people brought their sick to Peter that *even His shadow cast upon them might heal them* (Acts 5:15).

Polhill notes:

> "In the ancient world a person's shadow was the subject of much superstition and was believed to represent his or her power and personality, to literally be an extension of their person. Whether or not they were healed by Peter's shadow Luke did not explicitly say, but the note underlines the strength of the apostle's healing reputation."[16]

Such discipline reaped the reward of the first documented healing after Pentecost. From this dedication to prayer and the Word, Peter goes on to heal Aeneas from paralysis in Lydda, Acts 9:34, and raise Dorcas (Tabitha) from the dead, Acts 9:40. Miracles and signs continued to follow the apostles.

For those ministering, in every instance of healing, the power and pre-eminence of prayer is a consistent underpinning. Prayer and healing go hand in hand. We are in times now when demonstrations of healing will empower the testimony of Jesus forward that the world may see He is Lord. As you read this, ask God to give you the faith, boldness and compassion to reach out in prayer. Our job is to respond to the nudge. God can then move to accomplish His work.

6. BOLDNESS:

Acts 4:29, 31: *"Now Lord, look on their threats, and grant to Your servants that with all boldness they may speak Your word"...And when they had prayed, the place where they were assembled together was shaken; and they were all filled with the Holy Spirit, and they spoke the word of God with boldness.* (Also in Acts 2:29; 4:13; 5:29, 42; 9:27,29; 10:44-45; 11:15; 13:9-12, 14:3, 18:26; 19:8)

Boldness was a key characteristic of the faith-empowered Church. Shortly after Pentecost, Peter boldly stood with the eleven and *raised his voice* to address the crowds (Acts 2:14). Fearlessly, he proclaimed the reality of Jesus of Nazareth to the multitudes in the streets of Jerusalem. Luke records, *And with many other words He testified and exhorted them, saying, "Be saved from this perverse generation." Then those who gladly received his word were baptized; and that day about three thousand souls were added to them* (Acts 2:40-41). These were bold words to a very mixed and resistant culture. Such a stance required faith and assurance of the truth of the Gospel and of Jesus.

Much of Acts 4 relays the spirit of boldness in which the Apostles not only witnessed to people but faced opposition. Strong's definition of boldness, παρρησία parrēsia, relays the quality of being open, free in speech, confident and without ambiguity.[17] Such boldness characterized their speech before the Sanhedrin, Acts 4:5-12, and gave them favor with the people. Luke records the attitude of the crowds: *Now when they saw the boldness of Peter and John, and perceived that they were uneducated and untrained men, they marveled. And they realized that they had been with Jesus* (Acts 4:13). Trying to restrict them, the Sadducees commanded them not to use the name of Jesus. Peter and John refused saying: *Whether it is right in the sight of God to listen to you more than to God, you judge, for we cannot but speak the things which we have seen and heard* (Acts 4:19-20)—a bold and confident statement before people who were ready to beat them and throw them in jail.

Not only were the apostles bold in their speech; but they were bold in prayer. When they prayed, "Lord, You are God…" (Acts 4:24-31). Stott notes, "Their first word was *Despotes, Sovereign Lord,* a term used of a slave owner and of a ruler of unchallengeable power."[18] In other words, they called upon a God they knew was all-powerful, above all the challenges and circumstances they were encountering. Consequently, they were bold.

Such determination characterized their actions and drew the ire of the Sadducees. *Then the high priest rose up, and all those who were with him (which is the sect of the Sadduccees), and they were filled with indignation, and laid their hands on the apostles and put them in the common prison* (Acts 5:17-18). While in prison, an angel appeared opening the prison doors and instructed them to go back to the temple to teach. In spite of the resistance and threat of prison, they did not hesitate. Unhindered by fear, they stood in the temple and preached, *And daily in the temple, and in every house, they did not cease teaching and preaching Jesus as the Christ* (Acts 5:42).

They were also bold and discerning in confronting sin. In Samaria, Peter boldly confronted Simon, the sorcerer, saying, *"You have neither part nor portion in this matter, for your heart is not right in the sight of God. Repent therefore of this your wickedness…for I see that you are poisoned by bitterness and bound by iniquity"* (Acts 8:21-23). Jews largely avoided Samaria. The disciples were fearless in penetrating this highly resistant culture with the truth of the Word. Luke records, *So when they had testified and preached the word of the Lord, they returned to Jerusalem, preaching the Gospel in many villages of the Samaritans* (Acts 8:25).

In his journey to Philippi, Paul was fearless in confronting a demon-possessed slave girl, Acts 16:16. For many days, she followed Paul and harassed him and those that gathered around him. Finally, annoyed, Paul charged: *"I command you in the name of Jesus Christ to come out of her." And he came out that very hour* (Acts 16:18). As a result of setting her free, Paul was sent to prison and beaten with rods. Fearless, they faced the repercussions of a defiant and violent culture.

7. STRENGTH THROUGH JOY:

Acts 8:8: *And there was great joy in the city.* (Also in 5:40-42; 13:48-52; 15:3; 16:25; 20:24)

Corporate prayer is fun! The early believers experienced it! One of the outstanding characteristics of the Acts Church was its joy, even in the face of hardship and persecution. When Philip went down to the city of Samaria and preached Christ, multitudes heeded his teachings as they heard and witnessed the miracles he did. From deliverance of unclean spirits to healing the paralyzed and lame, Luke writes, *And there was **great joy in that city*** (Acts 8:8). Of note, there was joy even in the face of extreme conflict. Acts 13 records the journey of Paul and Barnabas to Antioch where the Jews strongly opposed them. They instead boldly turned to the Gentiles with the Gospel.

> *Now when the Gentiles heard this, they were glad and glorified the word of the Lord. And as many as had been appointed to eternal life believed. And the word of the Lord was being spread throughout all the region. But the Jews stirred up the devout and prominent women and the chief men of the city, raised up persecution against Paul and Barnabas, and expelled them from their region. But they shook off the dust from their feet against them, and came to Iconium. And the disciples were filled with **joy** and with the Holy Spirit* (Acts 13:48-52).

Despite the resistance and angst they received in Antioch, opposition spurred the disciples to spread the Gospel and did not steal their joy. What a lesson that is for us today as we face increasingly resistant cultures! This same strength of joy was exhibited by Paul and Silas when they were beaten and placed in the inner prison in Philippi. Where they would be expected to be weary and tired, Paul and Silas sang late at night. As a result, an earthquake erupted, and the shackles came off

---

their feet, and they walked out of prison. The quake was a power encounter!

Strongholds over Philippi broke the night Paul and Silas refused to give in to pain or hurt from their treatment. Its destiny as a city changed. Their joy broke through the demonic grip keeping them in prison and opened the opportunity to spread the Gospel. God supernaturally delivered them in the sight of the keeper of the prison. As a result, an entire family came to know the Lord.

They refused to leave Philippi unnoticed. As they did so, they left behind a legacy of a people who knew their God and rejoiced in Him always. It was a lesson that turned the tables of hate into love and gave people a chance to see the love and faithfulness of God. Paul later reflects on his experience in Philippi with these words,

> *"I thank my God upon every remembrance of you, always in every prayer of mine making request for you all with joy, for your fellowship in the gospel from the first day until now, being confident of this very thing, that He who has begun a good work in you will complete it until the day of Jesus Christ"* (Philippians 1:3-6).

Wherever the Word of God was received, there was celebration amongst the brethren. Luke states, *So, being sent on their way by the church, they passed through Phoenicia and Samaria, describing the conversion of the Gentiles; and they caused great joy to all the brethren* (Acts 15:3).

The quality of maintaining our joy in the face of opposition will be a vital tool to hone as times become more challenging. In nations both closed and open to the Gospel, resistance is rising. Learning to lean into the Lord and place our confidence and trust in Him will continue to be a challenge. However, in it, we will experience the "Joy of the Lord as our strength" (Nehemiah 8:10). In another instance, Peter and John endured a very tough trial and took a stiff beating in Jerusalem. Luke records their remarkable attitude:

---

*And they agreed with him, and when they had called for the apostles and beaten them, they commanded that they should not speak in the name of Jesus, and let them go. So they departed from the presence of the council, **rejoicing that they were counted worthy to suffer shame for His name.*** (Acts 5:40-41).

Is that our response to criticism? Is joy our response to people who misrepresent us or speak against us? Certainly, the example here is food for thought. Joy in God's messengers was key to the spread of the Gospel. It is what propelled strength and vigor in the early church to be strong and of good courage in the face of opposition. Such is the call and commission to us today as the world's systems increasingly become resistant to the message that we, as Christians, carry in our hearts.

SUMMARY:

Given the review of Acts, the dynamics of a healthy, vibrant corporate prayer community can be extracted. The following is a summary of the nature of the Acts prayer community. Engagement in the community was a strong cultural value in the early Church. In other words, their relational strength included:

1. They were **teachable and patient.** (Acts 1:4-7; Acts 2:44; 4:32-34; 12:5)
2. They **persevered** in prayer, being constant and of one accord. (Acts 1:12-14, 2:1,46; 4:24, 31; 5:12, 7:57, 8:6; 12:5)
3. They activated believers through **recognition and impartation**. (Acts 1:24-26; 6:6; 8:17; 13:3; 14:23; 15:40; 19:6; 24:23; 28:8)
4. They practiced **hospitality**. (Acts 2:42, 46-47; 9:43-10:48; 16:33-34)

5. The leaders modeled **faith-filled prayer.** (Acts 3:1-3; 5:12-16; 6:3-4; 8:4-8; 9:17-19, 32-35, 40; 14:8-10, 16:16-18, 25; 19:11-20, 23; 20:7-16; 28:1-9)

6. Prayer was **bold** and Kingdom-minded, penetrating culture through a clear concern for those around them. (Acts 2:29; 4:13, 29-31; 5:29, 42; 9:27,29; 10:44-45; 11:15; 13:9-12, 14:3, 18:26; 19:8)

7. **Strength through joy** yielded salvation and continued the spread of the Gospel, (Acts 5:40-42; 8:8; 13:48-52; 15:3; 16:25; 20:24)

Applying these principles to any corporate prayer expression will keep it healthy and active. The principles relayed through these letters to the seven churches are as viable today as they were when the letters were written.

After exploring the nature of corporate prayer, it is time to relay key biblical foundations of *why* corporate prayer is vital for the church's health. Understanding its import will lay the foundations for the reformation, re-thinking and re-prioritizing needed today for this crucial power engine of the Church. We will explore further what happens when corporate prayer is established and how it lays biblical foundations for the health of His Church, the spread of the Gospel and the advance of His Kingdom.

DISCUSSION QUESTIONS:

1. Which of the seven virtues of corporate prayer do you find most engaging? Which are challenging? Why?

    i. Teachable and patient. (Acts 1:4-7; Acts 2:44; 4:32-34; 12:5).
    ii. Persevering in prayer, being constant and of one accord (Acts 1:12-14, 2:1,46; 4:24, 31; 5:12, 7:57, 8:6; 12:5)
    iii. Encouraging of others (Acts 1:24-26; 6:6; 8:17; 13:3; 14:23; 15:40; 19:6; 24:23; 28:8)

---

iv.   Hospitable   (Acts 2:42, 46-47;   9:43-10:48; 16:33-34)

v.   Faith-filled (Acts 3:1-3; 5:12-16; 6:3-4; 8:4-8; 9:17-19, 32-35, 40; 14:8-10, 19-23; 16:16-18; 16:25; 19:11-20; 20:7-16; 28:1-9)

vi.   Bold for the Gospel (Acts 2:29; 4:13, 29-31; 5:29, 42; 9:27,29; 10:44-45; 11:15; 13:9-12, 14:3, 18:26; 19:8)

vii.   Joyful (Acts 5:40-42; 8:8; 13:48-52; 15:3; 16:25; 20:24)

2. What steps can I take to foster a closer relationship with God and with others?

3. How would you describe "Koinonia" in your own life with Christ followers? (Koinonia *fellowship* is first expressed in Acts 2:42 "And they continued steadfastly in the apostles' doctrine and *fellowship*, in the breaking of bread, and in prayers.")

PRAYER POINTS:

1. Pray for one another by asking God to use our strengths and to grow in our weaknesses.

2. Pray for practical steps you can take to engage with your local church or community to grow yourself and lend your strengths towards establishing corporate prayer.

ACTION STEPS:

Take action by making it a goal to encourage someone weekly by acknowledging their gifting and thanking them for how they have influenced or helped you. Pretty soon you will be making it a habit!

3

THE REASON: WHY CORPORATE PRAYER?

THE EMPOWERED CHURCH

When the Day of Pentecost had fully come,
they were all with one accord in one place.
Acts 2:1

C orporate prayer and worship are the time-honored power
engines of the Church. Throughout biblical history, corporate
worship and prayer propelled God's people into their purposes and
destinies. Understanding why Jesus emphasized His house to be a house
of prayer for all nations is essential for the revitalization and the
reformation of the Church today. One cannot deny the history-changing
impact of Pentecost in Acts 2:1, *When the Day of Pentecost had fully*
come, they were all with one accord in one place. Committed corporate
prayer literally birthed the New Testament Church. Dean Briggs
describes the Church, "As the governing arm of Christ, the ekklesia are
called to band together in prayer."[1]

The glory of the Lord filling Solomon's Temple is another case
where corporate prayer ignited a powerful outpouring of God's Spirit,
establishing the temple as a dwelling place of the Lord, 1 Kings 6:13,
8:10-11. Asa, Jehoshaphat and Hezekiah were all reformation kings of
Judah who restored *corporate* worship in the temple, eventually

---

yielding significant transformation for Israel, 2 Chronicles 14:2-5, 17:6; 2 Kings 18:4 respectively.

The temple was a place of corporate worship, at least for some time in the early life of the Church. Homes were a gathering place for smaller groups to fellowship and pray. Both played a vital role in fostering a culture of community in prayer. Stott remarks,

> "In his Gospel, he (Luke) says 'they stayed continually at the temple, praising God,' Luke 24:53, and in the Acts that in the room where they were lodging, 'they all joined together constantly in prayer in the home.' It was a healthy combination: continuous praise in the temple, and continuous prayer in the home."[2]

The temple was designed to be a *house of prayer,* Isaiah 56:7. It was the time-honored center of corporate worship and prayer for Israel through its long and tumultuous history. The Jewish dedication to corporate worship in the temple and fellowship at home fueled the new Church, establishing it as a dynamic force in the earth. John Polhill summarizes the quality of the early Church community from Acts 4: "The community life (of the Acts Church) is marked by four things: their unity in mind and heart (v. 32a); their sharing of their possessions (v. 32b); the power and witness of the apostles (v. 33a); and the grace of God, which rested upon them (v. 33b)."[3] Furthermore, Armin Gesswein relays insights through his queries on the Church today:

> "Why does the prayer meeting have such a priority? Why was it the first thing Jesus established when He built His church? When He left for heaven, why did He leave a praying congregation behind? Why was every member present there involved in 'prayer and supplication?' What motivated all the new members-by the thousands-to become prayer meeting members, and to do so at once? How could they raise and uphold this kind of a standard for every member? To ask such questions is to ask God for some of His greatest secrets for our congregations."[4]

Today, corporate prayer sessions have many expressions. They may encompass large global days of prayer in stadiums, or be as simple as meeting in homes, or rooms in businesses, schools, prisons or formed "Houses of Prayer." With the advent of COVID 19, these prayer communities have emerged to link nations through on-line, multi-participant virtual platforms.

As challenges to the Church will undoubtedly be mounting, in this chapter, we will look at how corporate prayer galvanizes the Body of Christ by unifying its diverse nature, mobilizing missions, catalyzing revivals, and empowering it through the work of the Holy Spirit.

CORPORATE PRAYER UNIFIES THE CHURCH:

The characteristics of the community of prayer in the early Church is expressed in passages such as Acts 1:14, *These all continued with one accord in prayer and supplication.* Or, Acts 2:42, *And they continued steadfastly in the apostles' doctrine and fellowship, in the breaking of bread, and in prayers.* Luke writes in Acts 4:24, *So when they heard that, they raised their voice to God with one accord.* At Pentecost, believers were together in "one accord." Such a community is a powerful tool in God's hands. Why? Because the Holy Spirit guides people into all Truth. This quality of "one accord" is mentioned eleven times in the book of Acts as follows: 1:14, 2:1; 2:46; 4:24; 5:12; 7:57; 8:6; 12:20; 15:25; 18:12; 19:29.

The word "accord" is ὁμοθυμαδόν homothymadon or, "of one mind meaning with one passion."[5] It connotes an image of an orchestra filled with different instruments but all harmonizing to the same tune. Strong's defines it: "The image is almost musical; a number of notes are sounded which, while different, harmonize in pitch and tone. As the instruments of a great concert under the direction of a concert master, so the Holy Spirit blends together the lives of members of Christ's church."[6]

34

Polhill further explains this characteristic, "The word translated 'with one accord' (*homothymadon*) is commonly used in Acts to express the unity of purpose and particularly applies to the "one heart and mind" (Acts 4:32) characteristic of the Christian fellowship (Acts 1:14; 2:1; 4:24; 5:12; 15:25)."[7] The picture of this corporate expression is not one of simple agreement, but instead carries depth and desire to be together. John Spina notes:

> "The word in Greek is ὁμοθυμαδὸν, which means literally "one or same mind". This word is only used 11 times in the New Testament, with Luke using it 10 times in the book of Acts. So Luke is telling us that the disciples were all of the "same mind" at this point, further stressing the idea of unity. He then says that the disciples were "devoting themselves to prayer." **In Greek, the word translated here as "devoting" is in the form of a present active participle, and is in the plural.** What this tells us is that this act of praying was something they were doing on a regular basis, not just something they did one time after they witnessed the Ascension."[8]

Despite witnessing the departure of Jesus through His ascension, they did not relent in prayer and stayed united in "one accord." In such a spirit of unity, the day of Pentecost finally came.

Luke describes, *When the day of Pentecost had fully come, they were all with one accord in one place* (Acts 2:1). This unique quality of one accord community in the Acts Church ignited people's hearts and propelled their actions forward. Such agreement wields a powerful force. No wonder the New Testament Church exploded onto the face of the earth. The quality of "one-accord" prayer permeated its meetings and gatherings. John explains this unifying nature: *That they all may be one, as You, Father, are in Me, and I in You; that they also may be one in Us, that the world may believe that You sent Me* (John 17:21). This Scripture relays the power of Christian unity as a witness to the world that God and Jesus are one.

———

It is notable that none of the prayers recorded in the book of Acts were focused on "me," or about the person or circumstance recorded in the Scripture. Their hearts were set on a pilgrimage to seek Jesus who became the unifier of a greatly diversified Church. From unschooled fishermen to a physician (Luke), and tax collector (Matthew), the disciples were unified by realizing their need and responding to their call to walk with Jesus. All prayers recorded in the book of Acts had an outward focus and concern for others leading to miracles and healings. Stott characterizes these prayers, "They persevered, and were of one mind."[9]

One-accord faith does not necessarily mean that there is agreement on every minor doctrine, but rather towards common concerns or needs, and that God has the answer. When the day of Pentecost came, they were all together in one place. Jesus was gone, so they assembled to pray knowing they needed power from on high.

Those gathered numbered a hundred and twenty, Acts 1:15. Stott notes, "In Jewish law a minimum of 120 Jewish men was required to establish a community with its own council; so already the disciples were numerous enough to form a new community."[10] At Pentecost, they were in one accord, but later Luke writes in Acts 4:32-33:

> *Now the multitude of those who believed were of one heart and one soul; neither did anyone say that any of the things he possessed was his own, but they had all things in common. And with great power the apostles gave witness to the resurrection of the Lord Jesus. And great grace was upon them all.*

The one-accord community was also mentioned in describing the Church in Samaria, *And the multitudes with one accord heeded the things spoken by Philip, hearing and seeing the miracles which he did* (Acts 8:6). The foundational part of the Church propagating its unity and expansion was ongoing community in prayer.

When people focus outwardly on their great need for God, one-accord prayer becomes the arrow that penetrates heaven, and God comes

———

down.   Whitsett notably states, "In corporate prayer the clergy/laity distinction dissolves in light of the awareness that all are part of the *laos* (people) of God."[11] We have witnessed the power of one-accord prayer in meetings where there is such level of agreement. Nations that are polar opposites in political and social issues have united together on common ground through Jesus Christ. There are streams of the prayer movement emerging that are engaging in corporate prayer and building community of worship/prayer together. Such movement is a positive sign.

J. Edwin Orr, historian of revivals, followed the four great outpourings of the Holy Spirit in the 19th century. He quotes, "There has never been a spiritual awakening in any country or locality that did not begin in united prayer."[12] In the wake of the American Revolution, 1776-1781, America's economy and moral condition was in a significant slump. Alcoholism had hit the streets, and bank robberies were a daily occurrence. Churches were losing members and colleges were populated with unbelievers. Orr continues:

> "The Methodists were losing more members than they were gaining. The Baptists said that they had their most wintry season. The Presbyterians in general assembly deplored the nation's ungodliness. In a typical Congregational church, the Rev. Samuel Shepherd of Lennos, Massachusetts, in sixteen years had not taken one young person into fellowship. The Lutherans were so languishing that they discussed uniting with Episcopalians who were even worse off. The Protestant Episcopal Bishop of New York, Bishop Samuel Provost, quit functioning; he had confirmed no one for so long that he decided he was out of work, so he took up other employment. The Chief Justice of the United States, John Marshall, wrote to the Bishop of Virginia, James Madison, that the Church 'was too far gone ever to be redeemed.' Voltaire averred and Tom Paine echoed, 'Christianity will be forgotten in thirty years."[13]

Amid the chaos, a man of prayer, Isaac Backus, responded to the call of God. When conditions were at the worst, he sent out an urgent plea for prayer for revival to every Christian denomination in the United

States. Churches responded, and an interlaced network of prayer meetings on the first Monday of the month began. Revival, the *Second Great Awakening,* and missions followed.[14]

CORPORATE PRAYER RELEASES MISSIONS:

Community and **committed corporate prayer** are foundational ingredients for the Church to fulfill its missional and Kingdom mandate "to make disciples of all nations" (Matthew 28:19). The Acts Church was missional. It was also a praying Church. Missions burst forth from the prayer room to the streets of Jerusalem and onto the nations. At Pentecost, Peter came out of the corporate prayer room, Acts 2:1, and stood up to preach in Jerusalem with the eleven, Acts 2:14. Luke records, *Then those who gladly received his word were baptized and that day about three thousand souls were added to them* (Acts 2:41).

Luke further characterized the Acts Church: *Continuing daily with one accord in the temple, and breaking bread from house to house, they ate their food with gladness and simplicity of heart, praising God and having favor with all the people. And the Lord added to the church daily those who were being saved* (Acts 2:46-47). George Peters, missiologist, wrote about Pentecost and the role of prayer and Holy Spirit in missions:

> "Pentecost becomes the watershed of a new type of world missions. As the outgoing God, the Holy Spirit transforms the centripetalism of missions into a dynamic and urgent centrifugalism.. The "Come!" is replaced by a "Go!" and the inviting voice of the priest at the altar is superseded by the herald rushing from place to place to call a people unto God."[15]

Paul, one of the greatest missionaries of the Bible, conveyed the value he placed on prayer-inspired missions through his writings. The apostle expresses his heart cry, *Brothers, my heart's desire and prayer to God for them is that they might be saved* (Romans 10:1). He wrote to the Ephesians exhorting them:

> *Take the helmet of salvation, and the sword of the spirit, which is the Word of God, praying always with all prayer and supplication in the Spirit, being watchful to this end with all perseverance and supplication for all the saints— and for me, that utterance may be given to me, that I may open my mouth boldly to make known the mystery of the gospel, for which I am an ambassador in chains; that in it I may speak boldly, as I ought to speak* (Ephesians 6:17-20).

These passages clearly relay the spiritual battle and the need to pray with focus and perseverance for the harvest.

Jesus modeled the life of prayer and missions. He spent his last night on earth with His disciples at the Garden of Gethsemane. Contending into the night, one can only imagine what He was praying about, or the dismay He felt at finding His disciple's fast asleep exclaiming, *"What, could you not watch with me one hour?"* (Matthew 26:40). Jesus knew He needed the Father's strength to carry out His mission. Fulfilling it would ultimately bring the Gospel to all creation, and thus the need for prayer.

Revival history and missions are linked to corporate prayer. The noted "Haystack Revival," was birthed by five unlikely college students who took a break from their studies at Williams College in Massachusetts on a hot Saturday afternoon in August 1806. They left to pray and discuss William Carey's "An Inquiry into the Obligation of Christians to Use Means for the Conversion of the Heathen."

Their discussion and prayer were interrupted by a hefty thunderstorm. Running to the nearest shelter, they took refuge in a nearby haystack. Samuel Mills, the group leader, had a deep passion for the Gospel to be spread to the nations. Continuing to pray amid the thunder and rain, the five eventually came to a joint, passionate agreement. Samuel cried out, "We can do this, if we will." Something broke at that moment in time. All five would point to that moment when God changed them forever. What became known as the "Haystack Prayer Movement" spread particularly through college students influencing missions for decades to come.

Mills would inspire the creation of several missions' organizations including the United Foreign Missionary Society, the American Baptist Missionary Union, and the American Bible Society.[16] Steve Hawthorne, mission/prayer mobilizer with Waymakers, reports in his review of the power of united prayer,

> "The 'first, and most important,' of the action points called for was 'fervent and united prayer…for the success of the gospel.' At a time when denominational fragmentation was great, Carey organized monthly prayer meetings to involve Christians of all denominations. Not long after Carey sailed for Serampore in West Bengal, India, the celebrated Haystack Prayer Meeting of 1806 in Williamstown, Massachusetts, positioned united prayer as the engine of mission mobilization in the United States."[17]

Today, by-and-large, the Church has drifted away from the engagement of prayer with missions. Studies, such as Barna Group's poll and study "Silent and Solo: How Americans Pray,"[18] clearly show a drift away from corporate prayer and, consequently its engagement with missions. Reporting less than 2% of the western church involved in corporate prayer and only 20% concerned towards global problems and injustices, the dynamic influence of corporate prayer in missions has been greatly sidelined.

Similar statistics were found in the *US News & Beliefnet Prayer Survey*. In their study, "The Prayer Practices of Christians, Jews, and Muslims," were evaluated. It is interesting to note that for Christians, 4.4% prayed in a house of worship, while 79.5% prayed at home.[19] The

---

home was also the preferred place to pray for Jews and Muslims, not in a corporate gathering place.

We are now in a time when Jesus is reawakening His Church to the importance of corporate prayer and worship in releasing the harvest. As times intensify, God is calling the Body of Christ to become the "house of prayer for all nations." The final frontiers of the global harvest loom. These frontline battles are gripped in the enemy's strongholds and require spiritual intervention in worship and prayer before the harvest is loosed.

In a review of "Finishing the Task," there are now 144 unengaged, unreached people groups of over 500 population.[20] This task is about to be completed to bring the Good News to every tribe and tongue. These people groups are locked in significant strongholds requiring the work of the Holy Spirit to break through the darkness and release the light of the Gospel. Francis Frangipane notes:

> "There are satanic strongholds over countries and communities; there are strongholds which influence churches and individuals....before victory can be claimed, these strongholds must be pulled down, and Satan's armor removed. Then the mighty weapons of the Word and the Spirit can effectively plunder Satan's house."[21]

Largely, this work is accomplished through the one-accord prayer of the corporate body of believers. George Peters wrote, "Reaching the unreached will, first of all, mean for us not only to lay hold of it in faith, but to develop thousands and thousands of prayer cells that will commit themselves wholeheartedly to prayer until the victory will be won."[22]

Whether it is the drug-addicted and homeless on our local streets or in the jungles of foreign nations, the end-time harvest is knocking at the door of the Church. Are we engaged with these frontiers in prayer? As times intensify, altars of praise and worship must be raised up to bring the necessary spiritual breakthrough to advance the Kingdom. God will not deny the cries of His people. It is the *one-accord* expression that will release the grip of strongholds and move hearts to reach the fields that are white with harvest.

CORPORATE PRAYER EMPOWERED THE CHURCH AND MIRACLES FOLLOWED:

Today, many believers go to church not realizing they *are* the Church. In the book of Acts, corporate prayer propelled the activity of the Holy Spirit throughout the community of believers. Sixteen of the twenty-eight chapters of Acts mention the Holy Spirit. Other chapters documented the work of the Holy Spirit moving in the works of the apostles and first Christians. God's supernatural interventions are recorded throughout the book.

Stott explains the power of the Holy Spirit in the early Church: "One thing is certain. Christ's church had been overwhelmed by the Holy Spirit, who thrust it out to witness."[23] Early church life was infused with the power that emanated from communities of committed prayer. Gesswein states, "The secret of all great revivals comes through right here in congregation power, because revival power is corporate power."[24] Whitsett states:

> "The early followers of Jesus routinely turned to corporate prayer and utilized it as a source of power and means of breakthrough when faced with overwhelming circumstances. They considered corporate prayer an essential element of the meaning of being a part of His body. From all evidence, it was woven into the fabric of their lives and regarded as an indispensable component of how their faith was expressed."[25]

Propelled by the release of the Holy Spirit at Pentecost, the disciples proclaimed the Gospel, praying and ministering to people. Subsequently, signs followed. Luke records, *And they continued steadfastly in the apostles' doctrines and fellowship, in the breaking of bread, and in prayers. Then fear came upon every soul, and many wonders and signs were done through the apostles* (Acts 2:42-43).

This was followed by continued demonstrations of the Holy Spirit's tangible and powerful impact. Luke records:

> *And through the hands of the apostles many signs and wonders were done among the people...Also, a multitude gathered from the surrounding cities to Jerusalem bringing sick people and those who were tormented by unclean spirits, and they were all healed* (Acts 5:12, 16).

Further examples of the Holy Spirit moving in great power are too numerous to mention here. From raising the dead to miraculous outreaches to both Jews and Gentiles, the Gospel spread, *And believers were increasingly added to the Lord, multitudes of both men and women* (Luke 5:14).

Stott relays the paradoxical result of such extraordinary signs: "The miracles had two interesting and opposite results...The presence of the living God, whether manifest through preaching or miracles or both, is alarming to some and appealing to others. Some are frightened away, while others are drawn to faith."[26] Such reactions strengthened the early Church's continued concern and prayer for those ministering.

Opposition only fueled the fire of the Church, such as when Peter was in prison during Passover. In Acts 12, he was arrested and thrown in a cell with two guards situated on either side of him and two at the doorway. However, "constant prayer was offered to God for him by the church" (Acts 12:5), at Mary's house.

While Herod decided to annihilate the Christians and kill Peter, an angel appeared to Peter, instructed him, and walked him out to the city gates that opened to them. Having been left by the angel, Peter immediately went to Mary's house to make a stunning appearance to all. Imagine the level of faith that was stirred that night in Peter and amongst the brethren in the community! Salvation, miraculous deliverance, and outpourings of the Holy Spirit were the result of these constant prayers.

As opposition increased, it must be noted that it did not deter the apostles and the early Church. It propelled them forward. In Jerusalem, the high priests commanded them not to teach in Jesus' name. Luke records their reaction: *But Peter and the other apostles answered and said: "We ought to obey God rather than men"* (Acts 5:29). After a severe beating in Jerusalem for preaching the Gospel against the ruler's command, Luke notes the attitude of Peter and the believers, *So they departed from the presence of the council rejoicing that they were counted worthy to suffer shame for His name* (Acts 5:41).

Again, while in Antioch, Paul and Barnabas received much favor from the Gentiles, but came under significant attack by the Jews. Luke relays their reaction: *But they shook off the dust from their feet against them and came to Iconium. And the disciples were filled with joy and with the Holy Spirit* (Acts 13:52). The result was the spread of the Gospel. Luke records a few demonstrations of such power as follows:

♦ *Now when the apostles who were at Jerusalem heard that Samaria had received the Word of God, they sent Peter and John to them, who, when they had come down, prayed for them that they might receive the Holy Spirit. For as yet He had fallen upon none of them. They had only been baptized in the name of the Lord Jesus. Then they laid hands on them, and they received the Holy Spirit* (Acts 8: 14-17).

♦ *While Peter was still speaking these words, the Holy Spirit fell upon all those who heard the word. And those of the circumcision who believed were astonished* (Acts 10:44).

Adversity propelled the Church and in fact, in many instances such as the angel releasing Peter from jail, became a conduit for God's supernatural intervention.

CORPORATE PRAYER IS A CATALYTIC FORCE FOR REVIVAL:

Revival history is replete with stories birthed out of the corporate prayer setting. There is not one revival recorded where corporate prayer was not a birthing center. In the 1700s a spiritual awakening broke open in multiple places across the nations. Such awakening largely originated through the corporate prayer expression that emanated from Herrnhut, Germany. Herrnhut, meaning "The Lord's Watch," became a birthing center influencing the awakenings that erupted in England and America.

Early in the 1700s, a community deeply divided by ethnic distinctions came under the leadership of Count Nicholas von Zinzendorf and began to pray together. Organizing into a twenty-four-hour time frame, the community launched 24/7 prayer with the addition of daily corporate prayer gatherings. The united prayer began to melt down the cultural differences, and people began to work together. Strivings began to cease. On August 13, 1727, the Holy Spirit poured out on the community and launched a prayer movement that lasted well over 100 years. Some credit this revival as a type of "Second Pentecost."[27] The seeds of the outpouring impacted people such as John Wesley. It fueled the awakenings during the "First Great Awakening," and which were experienced in other nations in the 1730s and 1740s.

The second great awakening in America began in Northampton, Massachusetts. Jonathan Edwards united God's people in prayer. Edward's pamphlet was entitled "An Humble attempt to Promote Explicit Agreement and Visible Union of God's People in Extraordinary Prayer for the Revival of Religion and the Advancement of Christ's Kingdom on Earth."[28] Such commitment to corporate prayer carries the reward of revival. It was so in the beginning and continues throughout Church history.

The third great awakening began in North Dutch Church in New York City. In the 1850s, America was enjoying great prosperity. However, morals had begun to decline and commitment to God waned. Jeremiah Lanphier, alarmed by the state of affairs, announced a prayer meeting for businessmen over the noon hour with the first one scheduled for the 23rd of September, 1857. Only a few showed up. But persisting through the disappointment, he knelt with the others and prayed.

After the third or fourth prayer meeting, panic struck. The financial markets collapsed, workers lost their jobs, and the economy tumbled. As the prayer meetings continued, they grew. By six months, more than ten thousand businessmen were meeting daily to pray during the noon hour. Talbot Chambers characterizes the meeting:

> There was no eloquent orator, no noted revivalist, no display of intellectual abilities, native or acquired; nothing to gratify a refined taste, or stimulate a jaded imagination, or cater to itching ears. It was simply a gathering of men who turned aside from secular cares to consecrate an hour to prayer. [29]

The first church and revival awakenings all had one thing in common: corporate prayer. It was a key to unlocking heaven's resources over countless communities small and large.

SUMMARY:

It can be safely extracted that corporate prayer was a foundational characteristic of the Acts Church and has been a catalyst for the revivals that have ensued over the centuries. Corporate prayer was a priority and directed the actions of the first believers and the missions of the apostles. It led to miracles and a bold stance in the face of opposition. The prophetic message of Isaiah 56:7 that His house is to be a "house of prayer for all nations" was a reality for the early church, Matthew 21:13, Mark 11:17, Luke 19:46. Consequently, the Acts Church experienced unity, missional desire, and power emanating from corporate prayer. Revivals that followed were all birthed in the womb of corporate prayer.

Communities of contending prayer are the power source fueling the engine of the Church through history. Such expressions are an instrument that has unified diverse groups of people, inspired dynamic missional movements, impacted the history of nations, and empowered believers through the work of the Holy Spirit. These are all important reasons why corporate prayer was central to the health and vitality of the early church, and it continues to be a conduit of God's desire for His body today. Understanding the biblical foundations of why corporate prayer is vital for the health of the church lays foundations for the reformation, rethinking, reprioritizing needed today.

DISCUSSION QUESTIONS:

1. What actions could you take today to engage in corporate prayer to foster God's purposes as explained in this chapter?
2. Of the results of corporate prayer described above, i.e. unity, release of missions, miracles, and revival, discuss what excites you the most and why?
3. How can you assist your local church community to make corporate prayer a priority? Identify action steps that will honor authority and build community.

PRAYER POINTS:

1. Pray for practical steps you can take to not only participate in but galvanize corporate prayer?
2. Ask God to give you compassion for the world around you.

ACTION STEPS:

1. Reach out and pray for someone in need of healing or assistance this week.
2. If you find yourself in negative, critical thinking towards yourself or others, ask God to give you His heart and compassion towards the issues.

4

THE REPORT: PRESENT DAY CHALLENGES

*Then they will deliver you up to tribulation and kill you, and
you will be hated by all nations for My name's sake. And then
many will be offended, will betray one another, and will hate
one another. Then many false prophets will rise up and deceive
many. And because lawlessness will abound,
the love of many will grow cold.
But he who endures to the end shall be saved.*
Matthew 24:9-13

Because corporate prayer is so critical for the health and vitality
of the Body of Christ, the enemy does everything possible to
keep it sidelined, away from the forefront of action plans, thereby
keeping the Church powerless. Community service and missions have
always been a functional part of the local church and vital to its life.
They may have worked in the past, however, today the power source
that moves us beyond the good to the God encounter will be increasingly
required to face the challenges ahead. Jim Cymbala comments in his
book *Fresh Wind, Fresh Fire*, "You can tell how popular a church is by
who comes on Sunday morning. You can tell how popular the pastor or
evangelist is by who comes on Sunday night. But you can tell how
popular Jesus is by who comes to the prayer meeting."[1]

Corporate prayer was integral to the New Testament Church.
Prayer was not an option; it was a way of life and essential for their

everyday sustenance. Jesus' life and teachings were pre-eminent in their culture. Throughout history, it has been the engine behind countless revivals. Banks notes: "Whenever something happens in the history of the church—whenever lives are transformed and revival occurs— people are praying together."[2] At the center of these revivals is a transformed heart, a heart that is not satisfied with things as usual, but earnestly desiring an encounter with God.

With the onslaught of COVID-19, congregational expression has been challenged. Is it essential? Is it necessary? Governmental intrusion on the separation of Church and State became a rigorous reality for many local pastors and leaders forcing a hard look at why and how we meet. Did it become a test on how hard do we, the Church, fight to gather physically? Was prayer involved? Was it a priority in the face of such a pandemic? These were questions that came to the forefront. Answers are still unfolding and in part, the incentive for this book.

In the present times of tumult and challenge, we will be tested to hold on to our faith as Christians. Jesus warns us in Matthew 24 of the trials that will befall the Church in the end-times. These trials are beginning to appear. The research released through Barna, "Silent and Solo, the State of Prayer in the American Church," conveys that people pray, but the corporate expression is lacking.[3] Other studies quoted throughout this book have also relayed this fact, Whitsett, Spina, Ridgaway, Polhill, etc. Through observation and ministry experience, this research corroborates the fact that corporate expression of prayer is by-and-large bypassed in the activity of the local church.

DEFINING THE PROBLEM:

Though it may be hard to swallow, research corroborates the sidelining of corporate prayer in today's Church. D. Edmond Hiebert poignantly states:

> "Prayer is the most powerful and effective means of service in
> the Kingdom of God ... It is the most dynamic work which

49

God has entrusted to His saints, but it is also the most neglected ministry open to the believer.

"The Bible clearly reveals that believing prayer is essential for the advancement of the cause of Christ. It is the essential element for Christian victory ...

"We may marvel at the spiritual power and glorious victories of the early apostolic church, but we often forget that its constant prayer life was the secret of its strength ...

"If the church today would regain the spiritual power of the early church, it must recover the truth and practice of prayer as a vital working force."[4]

Gesswein notes, "Churches today are not so much forsaking doctrine as forsaking assembling. It is one of the most serious problems in bringing about church renewal."[5] John Spina notes, "The American church today is in a poor state as it relates to the practice of corporate prayer. As I have had the opportunity to spend time in churches in several Asian countries, I have observed that our brothers and sisters in these other lands take corporate prayer much more seriously than do we in the United States."[6] As noted previously, the quantitative studies by Barna[7] and Ridgaway[8] reflect the relative lack of engagement of today's Western church with this biblical powerhouse.

Additionally, in reviewing the literature, finding the topic of corporate prayer is a challenge. There is a plethora of books, excellent qualitative and quantitative studies on the individual practice of prayer, history of prayer and revival; however, there is a relative lack of research on corporate prayer. Whitsett affirms this observation,

"The challenge of reviewing literature on the matter of corporate prayer is a difficult one because, while prayer in general has been a very popular focus of attention over the years and received wide treatment, the specific topic of corporate prayer has been largely neglected and overlooked."[9]

Though there is a plethora of quantitative and qualitative research and literature on personal prayer and prayer practices, what literature there is on corporate prayer supports the lack of corporate experience in the present-day Church (Barna, Ridgaway). In a General Social Survey in 2014, while "56.9% of people pray at least once a day, the corporate connectivity in prayer is largely lacking."[10]

If we understand why this historic cornerstone of the Church is largely ignored, or at very best significantly downplayed, we can begin to unravel the grip and release a new hope towards the recovery of this power-packed, first-Church expression.

A few examples are necessary as case-in-point illustrations. In his article/chapter "A Biblical Theology of Prayer," Edmund Clowney dissects various aspects of prayer. However, given the entirety of the review, only three brief paragraphs cover participation or influence in corporate prayer.[11] In his treatise, Clowney states: "God's covenant was never exclusively individual. At Sinai, all the people redeemed from Egypt entered into covenant with the Lord. Indeed it was God's covenant that formed a nation, a people of God, from the mixed multitude that came out of Egypt."[12] Though he acknowledges the importance of corporate prayer, it is not central to the theology of prayer presented.

In another instance, Richard Foster has written a book on prayer, *Prayer: Finding the Heart's True Home*.[13] It is an important book to equip our journey with the Lord. However, all chapters either focus on our personal prayer life and intimacy with God or praying for others. None of the chapters speak to the issue of corporate prayer. I would venture to guess that if you looked on your bookshelf, the books on prayer would largely be about individual prayer or spiritual formation with very few focused on corporate prayer. Personal intimacy with the Lord through worship and prayer is vital part to our spiritual growth; however, corporate expression carries its distinct weight and influence. Whitsett notes, "Most people see prayer as a me exercise instead of we."[14]

51

CHALLENGES TODAY:

CHALLENGES TODAY:

What has caused this relative slumber of the power engine of the Church? Centuries of Church history now gap between what we experience today and the Church in Acts. Several cultural issues have influenced this dichotomy between now and then.

In reviewing the literature, resistance to prayer—and particularly corporate prayer—rises from both within and outside the Church. Three distinct mindsets contribute to this inattention within the Body of Christ: individualism, secularism, and naturalism. Whitsett explains, "Today in North America, with its cultural undercurrent of individualism, secularism, and naturalism, prayer has largely become an individual pursuit to the detriment of corporate prayer."[15] These three influencers are noted by other authors as well and will be discussed in the ensuing sections. Challenges outside the Church include complacency fed by distractions and rising cultural resistance to the message and values of Christianity.[16] [17]

INSIDE THE CHURCH

INDIVIDUALISM:

Individualism takes its toll by convincing us that there is no need for the prayer meeting as long as people pray at home. Or it keeps us satisfied in our personal prayer times and relationship with the Lord. Whitsett explains, "Individualism is the cultural value that stresses the primacy and importance of personal goals to the exclusion of anything that would interfere with pursuing them wholeheartedly."[18]

As Christians, we can be intensely personal in our relationship with God, and the corporate expression can make us very uncomfortable. Surely, it is key to learn to "wait on the Lord," individually and to hear from Him. That is not the question here. The issue is whether we can expand our capacity to hear from Him and contribute our thoughts and insights to others in a corporate prayer environment.

As we hear from the Lord, individualism may also cause us to charge ahead…and come hell or high water, we are going to do it! It is a "Get out of my way," attitude, or "I am the one who has heard." That may be true, but how about allowing your revelation or insight soak in the waters of wisdom? There may be others who are to be involved, or who can lend insight. Although our personal prayer times are important, venturing forth through the door of corporate prayer can significantly enhance our private prayer life.

When I first received the vision for the Global Watch ministry, it was a powerful and life-changing encounter with the Lord (see chapter 9). However, it was something I pondered in my heart for a good fifteen years, before I brought it public. It took that long for God to train me and cultivate the vision through His Word. Eventually, the time came when it was released. I am thankful today that I did not rush off and start something I was ill prepared to do. So, if you are one where the vision seems to tarry, be encouraged! You are not alone. Habakkuk's words of wisdom are a comfort: *Write the vision and make it plain on tablets, that he may run who reads it For the vision is yet for an appointed time; But at the end it will speak, and it will not lie. Though it tarries, wait for it; Because it will surely come, it will not tarry* (Habakkuk 2:2-3).

When we move into the corporate setting, we begin to acknowledge and live out the great commandments Jesus taught:

> *"You shall love the LORD your God with all your heart, with all your soul, and with all your mind. This is the first and great commandment. And the second is like it: You shall love your neighbor as yourself. On these two commandments hang all the Law and the Prophets"* (Matthew 22: 37-40).

In this teaching, Jesus is relaying the value He places on our relationship with one another. Matthew records Jesus' words, *"For where two or three are gathered together in My name, I am there in the midst of them"*

(Matthew 18:20). This is a powerful statement. However, the importance of reconciliation is expressed in the preceding verses. Jesus gives us the protocol in resolving conflict. The process He relays reflects the value He places on the second commandment. If we walk in that protocol, and relationships are built and fostered, He promises to be in our midst (see Matthew 18:15-20).

As times escalate, we need the corporate prayer of agreement to help us breakthrough resistant spiritual atmospheres that are increasingly dark and difficult. Relational strength will be the conduit for powerful prayers that shift spiritual atmospheres. Centuries of denominational individualization have fractured the Church. Today, thankfully, a movement of watchmen is rising with hearts desiring to unite and build up the body of Christ (See Chapter 10). They carry eyes for God's covenant. They are moving beyond individual intercessory life or ministry to build relational connections and bridges to promote a oneness for healing of the nations. Isaiah declares, *Your watchmen shall lift up their voices, with their voices they shall sing together; for they shall see eye to eye when the Lord brings back Zion* (Isaiah 52:8). God is watching over His Word, and it will not return void.

SECULARIZATION:

Secularization is a term that "involves the historical process in which religion loses social and cultural significance."[19] Simply stated, when the Church secularizes, it loses its spiritual influence. This is a widely studied topic with different theories. From research done reviewing secularization, these characteristics are noted:

- ♦ Higher education and social differentiation will lead to a weakening of religion (Norris and Inglehart 2004).
- ♦ Modernization diminishes religious authority by minimizing risks, including physical, economic,

social and environmental threats and building up welfare states (Weber, 2003, and Durkheim, 2008). [20]

In other words, the more comfortable we become, the greater the propensity to fall into living in a secular narrative rather than living out biblical values. With COVID 19 challenging Church gatherings, has it become easier to stay home, do church on my own, and slip into the belief that it doesn't matter if I am a part of a larger church entity or not?

Whether COVID 19 or the constant demands of life itself, prayer is easily sidelined as we take on life's challenges and work them through our human capabilities. These attitudes are well expressed by Patterson, who explains:

> "Secularization, the process by which things like prayer are losing their practical social significance, is at the root of most of our difficulties with prayer. For many of us, on an almost subconscious level, there is a lack of confidence that something like prayer can actually get anything done...it makes us frenetically over-committed and so full of activity that we become too busy to pray."[21]

Whitsett corroborates this view noting that secularism propagates the idea "that anything of religious substance, while not necessarily harmful, is functionally irrelevant."[22]

Today, the world is replete with secular narratives driving the news. We are flooded daily with opinions and newsworthy items without foundations in the biblical narrative. Moving away from prayer, God's Word, and relationship with others, will move us quickly into agreeing and even seeking out the tree of knowledge. Climbing it will shift us seductively into secular narratives where the Bible and the values it espouses are lost in a sea of men's ideas or daily distractions without a solid biblical foundation to evaluate.

NATURALISM:

Closely related to secularism, naturalism nullifies prayer by explaining cause and effect. Results of prayer can be explained by natural causes, thereby disqualifying supernatural intervention in response to prayer. This influence, in particular, reflects a lack of faith in God's word. Clowney notes:

> "The assumptions of rationalism still underlie popular liberal thought. The physical universe is conceived as a machine governed by the laws of causality. It grinds on inexorably; it would be foolish to think that so insubstantial an entity as a whispered prayer could affect its course. Strangely, this view of nature is often supported by an appeal to God's laws."[23]

In days when knowledge is rapidly increasing, we can easily climb the tree of knowledge of good and evil and miss the message that is given through the tree of life. Daniel 12:4 gives a hint to the times we presently live in: *But you, Daniel, shut up the words, and seal the book until the time of the end; many shall run to and fro, **and knowledge shall increase*** (Daniel 12:4 emphasis added).

The knowledge this Scripture speaks of is *da'at.*[24] It is the word that describes the tree of *knowledge* in Genesis 2:17. It is a noun derived from the parent root "da" or דע (*da*). The meaning of the Hebrew letter ד is *dalet*, from the Hebrew word דלת (*delet*) meaning "door."[25] The letter ע is *ayin* meaning "eye."[26] According to Jeff Benner from the Ancient Hebrew Research Center, together these letters relay "the back and forth movement of the eye" as if reading, like the movement of a swinging door. "In the Ancient Hebrew mind, this careful examination is understood as knowledge."[27]

The verb *yâda* is derived from the same Hebrew root as *da'at and* means *to know.*[28] This word implies a special meaning and relationship with something or someone intimately. In Scripture, *yâda* relates knowledge to understanding God's character, His Word, and covenant. It connotes an intimate relationship as follows:

- *Now Adam **knew** his wife,* (Genesis 4:1).
- *For I have **known** him, in order that he may command his children and his household after him, that they keep the way of the LORD, to do righteousness and justice, that the LORD may bring to Abraham what He has spoken to him* (Genesis 18:19).
- *Do you **know** how the clouds are balanced, those wondrous works of Him who is perfect in knowledge?* (Job 37:16)

Naturalism easily flows out of the tree of knowledge/*da'at* of good and evil. *Yâḏa*, in scriptures, will take knowledge, *da'at*, and filter it through intimate relationship with God. Without experiencing the relationship with God and His Word in our lives, we can quickly turn to our natural reasoning rather than working through a more profound revelation and applying God's Word to our circumstances.

OUTSIDE THE CHURCH

COMFORTS, DISTRACTIONS AND COMPLACENCY:

The early Church lived in a hostile and oppressive Roman regime. Most of the apostles, except John, were martyred. In this resistant environment, the New Testament Church was birthed and flourished. The oppressive culture worked to ignite the Church and believers to draw them together. Desperation is a catalyst for prayer. On the other hand, distractions and lives of comfort can be significant deterrents to our personal and corporate spiritual health and well-being. Whitsett notes:

> "Given the preponderant affluence of the North American culture, Christ followers on this continent typically do not sense the kind of desperation that drives them to God or the

---

kind of hopelessness and distress that impels them to petition God corporately. As a result, corporate prayer has not been modeled or intentionally practiced. Additionally, the lack of emphasis on corporate prayer in twenty-first-century North America can be traced to a loss of awe for the holy that is subverted by thought patterns that mirror the surrounding society."[29]

Banks offers insight into this relative neglect of corporate prayer in the American church:

"It may be no coincidence that the culture we live in has become increasingly indifferent and even hostile to Christianity at the same time that united prayer has gone out of the church. As recently as fifty years ago, prayer meetings were a vital part of many churches. As American culture became increasingly entertainment oriented, the mid-week prayer meeting was replaced by the Wednesday night service. The active work of prayer was replaced with passive listening as the focal point shifted from God's power to answer prayer to what was happening at the front of the church. **Eventually the prayer meeting moved out of the sanctuary and into a corner of the church library. At the same time, the church's impact upon the culture around us began to decline**."[30] (Emphasis added.)

In the frenetic pace of today's world, distractions continue to lure us deceptively and vie for our attention. If not determinedly dealt with, they will fuel complacency and turn hearts away from God and His life-sustaining force within us. A.W. Tozer wrote, "To desire revival…and at the same time neglect personal prayer and devotion is to wish one way and walk another."[31]

Though we enjoy our comfort zones and routines of daily living, God is the great disrupter when He determines to move. COVID 19 has disrupted the nations of the world. Caught in the crossfires of pandemic and governmental restrictions, the Church has been squeezed out of its

---

58

four walls. The value of prayer is beginning to get highlighted. One study reviewing daily data from Google during the pandemic found searches for prayer in 95 countries surged to the highest level ever. Searches spanned all levels of income. The rise was due to an intensified demand for religion in the face of adversity.[32] God has given many in the Western nations great gifts of creativity, success, financial security. These are all gifts that must be stewarded, lest they be taken for granted and cause hearts to become complacent and spiritually inattentive.

Lack of corporate prayer reflects the heart's priorities. Whitsett notes, "In some ways the failure of the North American Church to give itself to corporate prayer can be viewed as an expression of dwindling compassion and a breakdown of love."[33] In the frenetic pace of today's culture, disciplined prayer life is hard to come by. At the core of this distraction are our individual and corporate priorities. The issue is not time, but rather our priorities. The psalmist states it well,

> *One thing I have desired of the LORD,*
> *That will I seek: That I may dwell in the house of the LORD*
> *All the days of my life,*
> *To behold the beauty of the LORD,*
> *And to inquire in His temple.*
> *For in the time of trouble He shall hide me in His pavilion;*
> *In the secret place of His tabernacle*
> *He shall hide me; He shall set me high upon a rock.*
> *And now my head shall be lifted up above my enemies all around me;*
> *Therefore I will offer sacrifices of joy in His tabernacle*
> (Psalm 27:4-6).

Jesus had hot words of warning regarding complacency in the letter to the Church in Laodicea, "So then, because you are lukewarm, and neither cold nor hot, I will vomit you out of My mouth" (Revelation 3:16). This is a stiff reprimand; however, we must realize we are now in a necessary awakening. The birth pangs of war, rumors of war, natural disasters, persecution of Christians are rising. Why?—Because God is removing the stumbling block of complacency out of His Church.

The comfort in this concern is that if you are facing certain trials, be encouraged! James writes, *My brethren, count it all joy when you fall into various trials, knowing that the testing of your faith produces patience. But let patience have its perfect work, that you may be perfect and complete, lacking nothing* (James 1:2-4). The tests and trials that will surely come are God's way of awakening the Church. It will be a process, but Jesus will have His spotless and passionate Bride.

CULTURAL RESISTANCE:

We are in a time when Christian values are being hotly contested. Standing up for what we know is right is being met with increased resistance and unveiled contempt in the Western world. In other nations, outright persecution continues to threaten Christians desiring to walk out their life's callings and values. Today, there is increasing pushback for Christians speaking up for their beliefs. Barna has studied Christians' and their views on their impact on culture:

> "Catholics, evangelicals, and mainline churchgoers, a majority say they feel misunderstood (54%), and persecuted (52%), while many others use terms like "marginalized" (44%), "sidelined" (40%), "silenced" (38%), "afraid to speak up" (31%), and "afraid to look stupid" (23%) to describe living their faith in today's world.

> Millennial practicing Christians, in particular, are getting hit from all sides. They are more likely than other practicing Christians to feel the negative repercussions of their faith. Most feel persecuted (60%) and misunderstood (65%), and almost half (47%) say they feel "afraid to speak up." In addition to millennial practicing Christians, evangelicals are just as likely to perceive their experience of faith in culture in these negative terms. They feel equally as misunderstood

(65%) and persecuted (60%) as millennial practicing Christians, and even feel slightly more silenced (50% compared to 46%) than their younger counterparts. Both groups report *relatively* higher than average numbers compared to the rest of the faith segments represented."[34]

An increasingly resistant environment will challenge our personal and corporate Christian values and life. Pew Research tracks harassment against religious groups worldwide. They reported, "Christians were harassed by governments or social groups in a total of 128 countries in 2015-more countries than any other religious group."[35]

In another study, Pew observed, "Government restrictions in 2018 were at their highest level since 2007."[36] They observed that the number of countries with "high" or "very high" levels of government restrictions is on the rise. 56 of 198 countries followed fall into these categories.[37] That is a whopping 28% of nations resistant to Christian values!

However, they also noted that, due in part to the large number of Christian-majority countries, Christians were actually harassed mostly in Christian-majority countries.[38] These facts reflect the need for vibrant prayer lives both personally and corporately in *all* nations. Fighting cultural resistance will be a continued challenge for the Church. As our surroundings become more resistant, the pressure to pray in agreement with one another and depend on God will only increase.

SUMMARY:

As a result of these influences: complacency, individualism, secularism and naturalism, corporate prayer—the biblical powerhouse of God's people—has been largely sidelined. Lewis O. Thompson is blunt in his assertion: "In many a church, the prayer-meeting is looked upon as a fifth wheel to its machinery."[39] This relative lack and neglect of corporate prayer reflect the priorities of today's Church.

However, the battle to reestablish corporate prayer is worth the effort. Whitsett states: "Corporate prayer, by its very nature, unleashes possibilities and opens the door to prospects that would otherwise remain untapped. It provides a channel and outlet for the longing to participate in purposeful, significant activity embedded deep within each person."[40] We will investigate how the transformation of the heart of the Church can take place by looking into God's Word and Jesus' message to the seven Churches of Revelation. They hold keys to unlock and unleash the end-time glory of the Church.

DISCUSSION QUESTIONS:

1. Take a moment and reflect on the influences found in our world today, as outlined in this chapter: complacency, individualism, secularism and naturalism. How have these influences invaded your own life? Respond to the Lord as the Holy Spirit prompts you.

2. By identifying these cultural deterrents what action steps can you take to overcome them?

3. How can you build relationships in your local community, particularly with those with whom you may have disagreements or conflict?

4. After reading the data displayed above, what "call to action" do you sense the Holy Spirit pulling out of you?

PRAYER POINTS:

1. Pray for one another in how to overcome the cultural influences that keep us separated from God and from one another.

2. Ask forgiveness for any gossip or slander that you have allowed to enter your ears or have spoken.

ACTION STEPS:

1. Make it a point to encourage someone today in their walk with the Lord.

2. Is there someone you have conflict with? Read Matthew 18:15-20 and take steps to reconcile.
3. Make it a daily habit to bless those who have hurt you or in whom you have conflict, "But I say to you, love your enemies, bless those who curse you, do good to those who hate you, and pray for those who spitefully use you and persecute you, (Matthew 5:44).

5

THE RESET: LESSONS FROM THE 7 CHURCHES

He who has an ear, let him hear
what the Spirit says to the churches.
Revelation 2:7, 11, 17, 29; 3:6 13, 22

The importance of corporate prayer expression cannot be underestimated. Through it, the first Church was born. Their prayers were from hearts that showed compassion towards one another, were Kingdom-minded, and were unrelenting in the face of a hostile, oppressive culture. Despite all the resistance, they were able to expand the Kingdom greatly.

As we have seen, corporate prayer practice is not the norm today. Akintunde contends, "Because of prayerlessness, the Church is not experiencing the move of God in terms of the revival, spiritual awakening and high rate of conversions witnessed during the time of the early Church."[1] He further asserts, "If the Church fails to pray and persist in prayerlessness, then she is not following the Master's instruction to pray at all times, Luke 18:1, 1 Thessalonians 5:17."[2] Sacks notes, "Having a praying church is not just a good idea; it is the foundation from which everything else flows."[3]

In biblical history, the Israelites journeyed through cycles, moving from their Abrahamic roots in Ur to the land deeded them by God, to Egypt, and back to the land promised them. Israel's history is rife with stories of straying and returning to the Lord. Such cycles can be readily identified in our personal and corporate lives today. The vitality and stability corporate prayer infuse into the Church cannot be underestimated. Its biblical origins, carefully laid out in the book of Acts and throughout the Scriptures, convey the importance of the practice for our spiritual growth and direction today. God is turning hearts back to the foundations upon which His Church, His Ekklesia, was birthed.

There is hope on the horizon. In a day when the Church needs to be a light in ever-increasing darkness, God is at work restoring this foundation to the Church. David Kinnamon, Vice President of Barna Research and director of the research for young pastors, studied millennials' spiritual practices. He notes a turning and desire for spiritual depth and prayer are rising in the Church. He states that churches "will find it very difficult to appeal to young people who deeply desire relational authenticity, service to the poor and disadvantaged, globally-minded activity, and spiritual depth through prayer."[4] This observation of a growing spiritual thirst is a herald to turning the heart of the Church and breaking the cycle of complacency. It has been my observation as well; there is a groundswell of desire emerging mainly in the prayer movement. As it influences the Body of Christ, it is hopeful that the heart of the Church will turn.

Additionally, today, we are facing the last frontiers of the global harvest. The remaining unreached people groups, including the homeless and drug-addicted on our city streets, are held back by strongholds that must be addressed through spiritual intervention before the fruit of salvation is fully gleaned. It will be challenging to reach these people without focused prayers of agreement from the body of Christ. Such invitations for God's intervention will facilitate the needed breakthrough to release the harvest, much like the Acts Church. Cheryl Sacks explains, "God's will can be accomplished when the church meets for prayer. 'The prayer gathering enlarges the channel through which God will bless and give victory to His people; it actually moves us into an entirely different realm of power."[5]

John's letter to the seven churches in Revelation lends a context for reviewing the Church. Though written to actual churches, the implications carry insight and warning for the believers today. The seven churches can represent four different things:

+ Seven literal churches which existed at the time Revelation was given.
+ Seven types of churches which can exist at any time in history.
+ Seven types of churches which will exist in the Last Days.
+ Seven types of individual believers.[6]

The implications of these letters reflect Jesus' heart and love for His Church. This review is not to be comprehensive but rather focused on what Jesus said and its application for today. Two of the five churches, Smyrna, and Philadelphia were found to be without fault. The remaining ones carry exhortations to the Church, not only applicable to the times when written, but today as well. We will examine the warnings and the strengths and attempt to apply them to our corporate expression today.

CHURCH AT EPHESUS: LOSS OF FIRST LOVE

Ephesus was a bustling port city, the center of a major trade route, and the capitol of the Roman province of Asia. As a center for trade, it was in a strategic location to promulgate the Gospel. It was also a center for pagan worship. The main temple was a huge statue of Diana, the goddess of the moon, childbirth and the hunt. Priscilla and Aquilla brought Christianity there in AD 52, Acts 18, and Paul spent two years there on his second missionary journey discipling and instructing the church elders. He met strong resistance from Artemis' followers led by Demetrius (Acts 19).

Given its location and emphasis in the Scriptures, it was likely a pre-eminent church in the region. Because of its inherent strength and influence, Paul warns the Ephesians in a letter written from Macedonia to "take heed" and to "watch" for "perverse things" (Acts 20:27, 31). The book of Ephesians describes the full armor of God and its

66

importance for believers to apprehend and wear in order to "withstand the evil day" (Ephesians 6:13). In 1 Timothy 1:3, he exhorts Timothy, who is in Ephesus, to deal with false teaching.

The next time we read a letter to the Ephesians is in the book of Revelation. It is from Jesus, as He addresses the Church. He commends their labor, patience, and perseverance. They have done many good works and had "not become weary" (Revelation 2:3). They had tested and exposed false teachers and those who lacked integrity (v. 6). However, in their labor He has one thing against them: they had lost their "First love," (v. 4) What does that mean? What is "First love?"

Jesus declared: "*'You shall love the Lord your God with all your heart, and with all your soul, and with all your mind. This is the first and great commandment.' And the second is like it: 'You shall love your neighbor as yourself.' On these two commandments hang all the law and the Prophets"* (Matthew 22:37-40). Wrapped up in good works, Jesus was warning them of losing their first love, the source of their love which is Jesus—God is love.

The picture being painted is an influential church filled with good works, but the catalyst for the good works is in danger of running dry. Why? Because they had lost their first love—their love for Jesus. God is love. This is a warning that our devotion will suffer without Him, and we can easily be engulfed with the busy distractions of work—even good works—that command our attention. In his article on "Restoring First Love," Adam Greenway says it well: "If we have the right love, then everything else falls into place."[7]

Summary:
- ♦ Affirmation:
    - o They were not lazy and were very involved in doing good works.
    - o They had exposed false teachers doctrines (false apostles, v. 2; the Nicolaitans, v. 6).
    - o They had persevered through difficulties.
    - o They had exhibited patience.

♦ Accusation:
  o They had lost their first love.
♦ Assurance
  o To him who overcomes, Jesus will give to eat from the tree of life from which all the fruit of God's goodness grows, Revelation 22:2.

Scriptures to meditate on:

♦ Proverbs 8:17: *"I love those who love me, and those who seek me diligently will find me."*

♦ Ephesians 3:15-19: *That He would grant you, according to the riches of His glory, to be strengthened with might through His Spirit in the inner man, that Christ may dwell in your hearts through faith; that you, being rooted and grounded in love, may be able to comprehend with all the saints what is the width and length and depth and height— to know the love of Christ which passes knowledge; that you may be filled with all the fullness of God.*

♦ John 15:9: *"Just as the Father has loved Me, I have also loved you; abide in My love."*

Application:

God desires a relationship with us. Prayer is the conduit through which we can experience His Presence, love, and hear from Him. The Ephesian Church was full of good works, perseverance, and faithfulness—all wonderful attributes for today's Church. They also experienced sound teaching by not receiving that which was false.

However, Jesus' concern was the loss of their first love. Prayer is first and foremost about a relationship with God. It is the vehicle of communication between God and us. Like any friendship, listening plays an important role, and that holds for communication with God. Every letter to the seven churches has the words "He who has an ear," (Revelation 2:7, 11, 17, 29; Revelation 3:6, 13, 22). In this letter, Jesus lays an essential foundation and exhortation for the rest of the Churches.

He desires connection with us so we can commune with Him, know Him, and not only talk to Him but listen and hear. Our personal and corporate prayer life reflects that desire.

CHURCH AT SMYRNA: PERSEVERANCE AND FAITHFULNESS IN TRIBULATION

Smyrna was a church almost the opposite of Ephesus. As a port city some thirty-five miles up the coast from Ephesus, it was a large commercial export center. It received its name from one of its principle commercial exports, Myrrh, which means *bitter*. As a Roman ally, the city was a key center for emperor worship.

In his commentary on Revelation, Tom Lowe notes, "The famous 'Golden Street' traversed the city with a temple to 'Zeus' at one end and the temple of a local goddess Sipylene (Cybele) at the other. Other Temples to Apollo, Asclepius, and Aphrodite lined the way."[8] The Church itself was likely founded by Paul or one of his leaders during his stay in Ephesus, Acts 19:10. The emperor Nero had died, and a new emperor, Domitian, was on the throne. His rule would prove to be harsh, and persecution in the area would last over two hundred years. It became a city marked by a bloody history.

One of the most notable martyrs was Polycarp. A disciple of John, Polycarp had been warned of his head being burned in the fire three days before his death. When arrested, he fed his captors and asked to pray for one hour. He prayed in front of those who had come to arrest him for two hours. By the end, his captors were remorseful over their task. Nevertheless, he was taken to the city, tried, and went through a brutal martyrdom, never once denying Jesus.[9]

Despite its history, Smyrna was one of the churches with which Jesus found no fault. Through John's letter, Jesus was warning of coming persecution, and presenting Himself as, "The First and the Last, who was dead, and came to life" (Revelation 2:8) referring to His resurrection. The oppression was overt from a harsh government, and from the Jews in their region. Jesus urged them not to fear. He said though they were poor, they were rich, and commended their perseverance and ability to overcome. Despite the affliction they would endure, He encouraged them, "Be faithful until death, and I will give you the crown of life" (Revelation 2:10). The modeling of this church is important for today as Christianity becomes more tested and believers are increasingly persecuted for their faith.

Summary:
- Affirmation:
    - Faithful at all times, even through persecution.
    - They were overcomers.
- Accusation:
    - None.
- Assurance:
    - They shall not be hurt by the second death.

Scriptures further exhort us today:
- 1 Peter 1:6-7: *"In this you greatly rejoice, though now for a little while, if need be, you have been grieved by various trials, that the genuineness of your faith, being much more precious than gold that perishes, though it is tested by fire, may be found to praise, honor, and glory at the revelation of Jesus Christ, whom having not seen you love."*
- James 1:2-4: *"My brethren, count it all joy when you fall into various trials, knowing that the testing of your faith produces patience. But let patience have its perfect work, that you may be perfect and complete, lacking nothing."*
- James 1:12: *"Blessed is the man who endures temptation; for when he has been approved, he will receive the crown of life which the Lord has promised to those who love Him."*

- Galatians 6:9: *"Let us not lose heart in doing good, for in due time we will reap if we do not grow weary."*
- Hebrews 10:36: *"For you have need of endurance, so that when you have done the will of God, you may receive what was promised."*

Application:

The Church in Smyrna is without fault. It thrived in dark, resistant and violent cultures. We all hear about persecution in closed nations such as Iran, Syria, and other Islamic-controlled countries. Yet, Iran is noted as having one of the fastest-growing churches in the world. Much has to do with the intensity of the discrimination. In many ways, particularly when in agreement corporately, such oppression can be a catalyst for church growth, as people gather to strengthen one another in the Lord.

As Western culture is becoming increasingly resistant to biblical values, corporate prayer meetings will become more central to Christian life and the Church. To support this, a recent study in church/state relations on Christian population growth found, "Persecution can, paradoxically, sometimes strengthen Christianity by deepening attachments to faith and reinforcing solidarity among Christians."[10] Conversely, "Countries where Christianity is privileged by the state encourage apathy and the politicization of religion, resulting in a less dynamic faith and the overall decline of Christian populations."[11]

The New Testament Church was birthed in a resistant, violent culture. Its growth continues to be spurred by trials and resistance, causing our hearts and minds to turn back to God and be strengthened by one another.

THE CHURCH AT PERGAMOS: THE COMPROMISING CHURCH

For two centuries, Pergamum served as the capitol of the Roman province of Asia. After Attalus III bequeathed it to Rome in 133 BC, it became a chief cultural and intellectual center. John's letter describes it

---

71

as the "seat where Satan's throne is" (Revelation 2:13). Interestingly, Steve Sewell notes about Pergamum:

> "It is an old tradition, that, as the papyrus plant had not begun to be exported from Egypt (Kitto), or as Ptolemy refused to sell it to Eumenes (Prof.Stuart), sheep and goat skins, prepared for the purpose, were used for manuscripts; and as the art of preparing them was brought to perfection at Pergamos, they, from that circumstance, obtained the name of "pergamena" or "parchment."[12]

Famed for producing products for the written word, i.e. parchment, Jesus relays Himself as, "He who has the sharp two-edged sword" (Revelation 12:12). The two-edged sword is the "Word of God," Hebrews 4:18. Those in Pergamum reading this letter would have had significant insight into Jesus' inference.

Jesus tells the Church at Pergamos that He knows their plight, the hostile environment in which they live, and its inherent dangers. He knew about the martyrdom of Antipas, a faithful believer martyred in their city, and applauds their faithfulness amid a dark and evil culture. However, Jesus holds a few things against them—namely, the doctrine of Balaam, and that of the Nicolaitans.

Long story short, the doctrine of Balaam gave license to the Jews to commit fornication and worship gods of other races. More than likely, the pagans of Pergamum were encouraging Israelites to join in their pagan feasts.

The Church at Pergamum also allowed the doctrine of the Nicolaitans to creep in. The word Nicolaitans means to "Nullify" the "Laity." In other words, its ultimate purpose separated believers from their full inheritances in Christ to disqualifying—or nullifying—their identities. The Nicolaitans misused the grace of God by believing "that a person is saved by grace and therefore it doesn't matter how you live."[13] Jesus hated the doctrine. It placed human reasoning and knowledge above the Word of God.

72

It could be reasonably extracted that the Pharisees and Sadducees were living examples of the Nicolaitan spirit in Jesus' day. They may not have lacked knowledge, but their application lacked love, thus separating themselves from the lives of the Jewish people.

Because of the shallowness of their relationship with God, their knowledge of His Word and love suffered. This lack deprived the Church in Pergamum of the discernment necessary to keep such doctrine from influencing them.

Summary of the Church of Pergamum:
- ♦ Affirmation:
  - o They held fast the name of Jesus.
  - o They did not deny their faith.
  - o Antipas was a faithful witness and martyr for Christ.
- ♦ Accusation:
  - o They succumbed to the influences of the world by committing fornication and eating food sacrificed to idols.
  - o They lacked discernment in doctrines they embraced.
- ♦ Assurance:
  - o To him who overcomes the influence of the world, Jesus would give the hidden manna, revelation of His Word.
  - o Jesus will give a white stone that only the one holding it knows. This stone could very well represent one's identity in Christ. It is given personally by Jesus to hold, and "No one knows except him who receives it" (v. 17).

Scriptures:
- ♦ 1 Timothy 4:6-7: *If you instruct the brethren in these things, you will be a good minister of Jesus Christ, nourished in the words of faith and of the good*

---

doctrine which you have carefully followed. But reject profane and old wives' fables, and exercise yourself toward godliness.

- Romans 10:17: *So faith comes by hearing, and hearing through the Word of God.*
- Hebrews 11:1: *Now faith is the substance of things hoped for, the evidence of things not seen.*
- John 14:23 *"If anyone loves Me, he will keep My word; and My Father will love him, and We will come to him and make Our home with him."*

Application:

In this letter, Jesus appears as the one who has the sharp, two-edged sword meaningfully wielded as the Word of God in Hebrews 4:12 and Ephesians 6:17. Scriptures are a vital instrument in prayer. Without God's Word working through our lives, and in particular our prayers, we can quickly fall into traps and false doctrines as those in Pergamum did. Today, conspiracy theories and deception are on the rise across the globe. Isaiah prophesied, *Woe to those who call evil good, and good evil; who put darkness for light and light for darkness* (Isaiah 5:20). We are distinctly in times when the Word of God must become that Hebrews 4:12 doubled-edged sword in daily actions.

Some examples of the character and nature of the Word of God:

- It is creative, Genesis 1:3; 2 Peter 3:5; Colossians 1:15-17; 2 Corinthians 5:17.
- It is proven, 2 Samuel 22:31.
- It guides, Psalm 119:101, 133; 1 Timothy 6:9.
- It is truth and yields life and light, 1 Kings 17:24, Psalm 119:105, 130; John 8:12.
- It is pure, Proverbs 30:5, Psalm 119:140; 12:6.
- It will not return void; Isaiah 55:10-11; Numbers 23:19.
- It is living, active, and powerful, pierces soul and spirit, and joints and marrow, discerner of thoughts, Hebrews 4:12; Romans 1:16.

- ◆ It is transformative, Romans 12:2.
- ◆ It is eternal, Psalm 19:8-9; 1 Peter 1:25; Luke 21:33.

By praying and declaring Scripture in private and corporate prayer, we can be assured that God is watching over His Word to perform it; and it will not return to Him void. The enemy cannot steal when the Word of God prevails and is proclaimed. He is a covenant-keeping God. His Word is Truth, as the psalmist writes, *My covenant I will not break nor alter the word that has gone out of My lips* (Psalm 89:34). Furthermore, *For the word of the Lord is right, and all His work is done in truth* (Psalm 33:4). By standing on the promises in God's Word, Satan cannot steal our attention and lead us astray.

THE CHURCH AT THYATIRA: THE CORRUPT CHURCH

Thyatira was a city in Asia Minor, also known as Pelopia. Though it was the smallest of the cities mentioned in John's letter to the seven churches, it received the longest letter. Cotton and a reddish root used for dying red were raised abundantly in the area. This area was noted for both the art of dying and for its textile, leather, and tanning products. Lydia, a seller of purple cloth, was from Thyatira, Acts 16:14.

Christians in Thyatira appeared to love Jesus. In this letter, He introduces Himself as the "Son of God." It is the only letter in which He uses that title. God was central to their lives and demonstrated their love through good works of service and were patient, or more literally persevered, Gr. *hypomonē*,[14] v. 19.

However, Jesus pointed to a person in their midst, Jezebel. Though famed as Ahab's wife in the Old Testament, (1 Kings 18, 19, 21; 2 Kings 9) this woman was different. She was a teacher. The Church leadership allowed teaching of false doctrine that ultimately led people into sin and they did nothing about it. Apparently, they were not strong enough to stand up to her.

One of Satan's traps is to lure people into doctrines that are subtly off track. Eventually permeating thought processes and becoming acceptable, such deception leads people into apostasy. The mention of a "bed" or "sickbed" is an allusion that there was sexual immorality involved in the teaching of Jezebel.[15]

Jesus tells the Church He searches the hearts and minds of men. He knows their innermost thoughts and desires: *"I am He who searches the minds and hearts. And I will give to each one of you according to your works"* (Revelation 2:23). To the faithful and those who overcome the distractions and lure of the deception, Jesus would give *power over the nations* v. 26. The Church had, and continues to have today, a powerful destiny to overcome the seat of Satan. The Ekklesia has been given "the keys of the Kingdom that the gates of Hades shall not prevail against" (Matthew 16:19)! To the faithful in this overcoming Church, He would give them "the morning star" v. 28. It is the brightest star in the sky and appears at the dawn of a new day. Interestingly, the Bible closes with Jesus declaration: *"I am the Root and Offspring of David, the Bright and Morning Star"* (Revelation 22:16).

In days of increasing darkness, our promise is that Jesus, our eternal hope, the bright and morning star, will one day light the horizon and darkness, and striving will pass away. As we remain faithful to His Word, may the "Maranatha" cry, "Come, Lord Jesus," feed the hope and the light within us.

Summary of the Church at Thyatira:
- ◆ Affirmation:
    - ○ Works of love, faith, service, and patience, v. 19.
    - ○ The last works were greater than the first.
    - ○ Not all of the church followed the teachings of Jezebel, or that of Satan.

- Accusation:
  - They allowed false teaching that lured them into sexual immorality and eating things sacrificed to Idols.
- Assurance:
  - To those who overcome, stand in integrity, and keep Jesus' works until the end, He will give power over the nations, v.26.
  - They will be given the morning star: the light and life of Jesus.

Scriptures:

- Romans 12:1-2 *"I beseech you therefore, brethren, by the mercies of God, that you present your bodies a living sacrifice, holy, acceptable to God, which is your reasonable service. And do not be conformed to this world, but be transformed by the renewing of your mind, that you may prove what is that good and acceptable and perfect will of God."*
- Hebrews 12:14-15: *Pursue peace with all people, and holiness, without which no one will see the Lord: looking carefully lest anyone fall short of the grace of God; lest any root of bitterness springing up cause trouble, and by this many become defiled;*
- 2 Corinthians 7:1: *Therefore, having these promises, beloved, let us cleanse ourselves from all defilement of flesh and spirit, perfecting holiness in the fear of God.*
- 1 Peter 1:14-16: *...As obedient children, not conforming yourselves to the former lusts, as in your ignorance; but as He who called you is holy, you also be holy in all your conduct, because it is written, "Be holy, for I am holy."*
- Matthew 5:14-16: *You are the light of the world, a city that is set on a hill cannot be hidden. Nor do they*

light a lamp and put it under a basket, but on a lampstand, and it gives light to all who are in the house. Let your light so shine before men that they may see your good works and glorify your Father in heaven.

Application:

As times escalate, this letter has significant meaning as an exhortation to be lights in an increasingly dark world. The Church has been called to be in the world but not of, or conformed to this world. Jesus said, *"My kingdom is not of this world,"* (Matthew 18:36). He also instructed, *"As You sent Me into the world, I also have sent them into the world"* (John 17:18).

We were created to influence our world, and guard our hearts against the world's influence on us. When light shines, it causes darkness to dispel. If we do not have a relationship with our Lord through prayer and His Word, darkness will abide. We will not be able to think or see clearly, and any spiritual influence will be dimmed.

As believers, we are called to bring light: not to conform to the darkness around us. Remember how Paul exhorted the Roman Church to continually renew their minds and not be conformed to present cultural pressures, *And do not be conformed to this world, but be transformed by the renewing of your mind, that you may prove what is the good and acceptable and perfect will of God* (Romans 12:2). Acquiring this attitude requires ongoing discipline and purposeful engagement with God in our personal and corporate lives as the body of Christ. Without a personal relationship with Jesus in prayer, the steady influence of the Word, and an engagement with others, it will be tough to keep our lamps burning.

The message to Thyatira was an appeal to the compromised Church. May God find us committed, not compromised, as pressures increase and the lure to retreat causes our light to grow dim. We are in times when the radiance of God's Truth will be tested. God desires for us to be those beacons and engage with the culture. Light will always conquer the darkness and people will be drawn to it. He is the One who watches over His Word and it will not return to Him void, Isaiah 55:11.

The Church at Sardis: The Dead Church

Sardis was a city known for its past wealth and splendor but had deteriorated greatly. Seated on a high hill with surrounding cliffs, it was considered impenetrable. It was once the capitol of the Lydian monarchy.[16] The earliest known ancient coin also came from Sardis. The money was made from Electrum, an alloy of silver and gold, found near the city.

Though seated high upon sharp cliffs and seemingly secure, the city was invaded twice, once by Cyrus in 546 BC and once by Antiochus the Great in 218 BC.[17] There was only one way of attack via a narrow path: "But the story goes that on one occasion the lookout (watchman) dropped a piece of armor. As he went to retrieve it, he inadvertently revealed the way up. Another story recounts how the guard simply fell asleep."[18] Whichever is true, the example of Sardis warns us of the dangers of becoming proud and over-confident of falling asleep while the enemy is waiting for the moment to attack.

Understanding Sardis' physical layout, wealth, and its seeming sense of security, makes the letter all the more meaningful for Jesus says, *"Be watchful and strengthen the things that remain, that are ready to die"* (Revelation 3:2). In other words, we can live a life that feels secure and comfortable. But what happens when our comforts become our way of life? We can be dangerously unaware of changes that God desires and our choices lead us to works that are dead.

A central theme of exhortation to this Church was to "watch." As a Church, they were filled with good works, but became self-reliant denying the real power of God. They had enjoyed a name that seemed alive, but it was empty. Jesus knows the thoughts and intents of the heart. In Sardis, they were found wanting. As such, Jesus instructed

———

them to be watchful to make sure the purposes of God were being fulfilled.

The Greek word grēgoreuō, watchful, means giving strict attention to, being vigilant and taking heed.[19]   The promise meant they would "walk with Me in white, for they are worthy" (Revelation 3:4). Wow! Being *watchful* leads to a lifestyle of *walking* with Jesus. This would be the only church that would have the privilege of doing that.

Jesus clearly exhorted this congregation, which thought itself dwelling in safety, to be watchful. He warns them that if they fail to do so, *"I will come upon you as a thief, and you will not know what hour I will come upon you,"* v. 3. In other words, they could not recognize what God wanted to do in their midst. Being *watchful* carries the key to life in the body of Christ, lest we become like Sardis...the *dead church.*

Jesus exhorted them to "remember" what they had been called to, v. 3. Remembering Jesus and being thankful for what He has done in our lives is an essential spiritual discipline. It becomes our testimony lest we forget and fall into the trap of complacency, lack of faith, humanistic effort, over-confidence, and reasoning. Jesus, therefore, exhorted them: "Be watchful."

His admonition was clear, and His call was, *"He who has an ear, let him hear what the Spirit says to the churches"* (Revelation 3:6). The counsel continues today. The call to watch and to pray was Jesus' last exhortation to mankind before the crucifixion, *"What! Could you not watch with Me one hour?"* (Matthew 26:41; Mark 13:33; 14:38; Luke 21:36). Why? Because He is coming for a ready and alert bride that knows how to watch and walk with Jesus.

Summary of the Church at Sardis
- ♦   Affirmation:
  - o   None.
- ♦   Accusation:
  - o   Their works were in name only.
  - o   Their works were dead.

- o Assurance:
- o To be watchful and overcome the defilement, pride, over-confidence around them.
- o To the faithful, you will walk with Jesus.
- o Jesus will recognize you before the Father and the angels and your name will not be blotted out of the book of life, Revelation 3:6.

Scriptures:

- ♦ 1 Corinthians 10:12: *Therefore let him who thinks he stands take heed lest he fall.*
- ♦ Matthew 26:41: *Watch and pray, lest you enter into temptation. The spirit is indeed willing, but the flesh is weak.*
- ♦ Mark 13:33: *Take heed, watch and pray; for you do not know when the time is.*
- ♦ Genesis 2:15: *Then the Lord God took the man and put him in the garden of Eden to tend and keep (watch) it.*
- ♦ Jeremiah 6:16: *Stand in the ways and see, and ask for the old paths, where the good way is, and walk in it; then you will find rest for your souls.*
- ♦ Matthew 25:23: *Well done good and faithful servant; you have been faithful over a few things. I will make you ruler over many things. Enter into the joy of your Lord.*

Application:

When uncontested, we can easily slip into a false sense of security. Such was the concern for the Sardis church. Given a position seated high on cliffs, they thought they were safe and secure. Two invasions proved them wrong.

On 9/11/2001 and today with the COVID pandemic striking the nations, our comfort zones have been rocked. When terrorists flew two planes into the twin towers of the World Trade Center in New York City on 9/11/2001, ramifications resounded across the nations sending all into an uncertain future. Likewise, the COVID pandemic spiraled us into challenges we have not faced before.

These are birth pangs of awakening. The wake-up call to watch and pray is being heralded. Comfort zones of slumber and sleep are becoming increasingly dangerous for our individual and corporate lives. Looming, is a great "falling away," 2 Thessalonians 2:3, for a largely prayerless Church.

God has given us each a garden to watch over. He is calling us to a higher level of attention and accountability as His stewards. We can no longer take for granted what He has put in our care, lest we find it dead and unfruitful in the future. This is an hour to take time to evaluate what is happening in our spiritual houses, individually and corporately, and ask God how we can more effectively tend and keep the garden He has given us.

THE CHURCH AT PHILADELPHIA: THE FAITHFUL CHURCH

Philadelphia was a city in Asia Minor situated on an important trade route. The area was surrounded by vineyards and became a wine-producing area. Populated by Jews, Christians and converts, it had the most extended Christian history. Located in an area that had many earthquakes, it was damaged by the shakings. In rebuilding, the rulers tried to change its name on three separate occasions, but failed. In modern times, Christians in the community have suffered under Turkish rule. Sewell notes, "Following the edict of the League of Nations in 1922, practically all the Christians were deported."[20]

The Church of Philadelphia was known as the city of "Brotherly love." Founded by two brothers, the name held throughout the ages. Jesus spoke Isaiah 22:22 over the Church. It was to have a key of David. What is the key of David? Mentioned only twice, it refers to authority, particularly over Jerusalem where the city of David remains to this day. Speaking prophetically then to believers, as well as believers today, God is searching for hearts committed to Him no matter the circumstances.

The Philadelphia Church earned a reputation of persevering even when they had little strength and "have not denied My name," v.8.

Thus, the key of David is powerfully significant. Those who opposed the believers, those from the synagogue of Satan, would eventually see this authority and see the beauty of God's love emanating from the congregation. Such a diligent pursuit of healthy, vibrant community life will protect them when God tests those who dwell on the earth.

Jesus cautions the Church not to allow others to take their crown. This is an interesting concept. "Crown" in Greek is *stephanos*, meaning a mark or wreath or garland given to victors. In other words, don't let someone steal or rob you of your value and your victory. Jesus will make those who hold steadfast pillars in the temple of God: *"I will write on him My new name"* (Revelation 3:12).

Summary of the Church of Philadelphia
- ◆ Affirmation:
  - o Though they had little strength, they have kept God's Word.
  - o They did not deny Jesus name.
  - o Do not let any take their crown.
- ◆ Accusation:
  - o None.
- ◆ Assurance:
  - o False Jews will worship before their feet.
  - o God will keep them from the hour of trial upon the earth.
  - o Whoever overcomes will be made a pillar in the temple of God.
  - o The name of God and Christ's new name will be written upon them.
  - o The term "New Jerusalem" will be written upon them.

Scriptures

- ♦ Colossians 3:12-14: *Therefore, as the elect of God, holy and beloved, put on tender mercies, kindness, humility, meekness, longsuffering; bearing with one another, and forgiving one another, if anyone has a complaint against another; even as Christ forgave you, so you also must do. But above all these things put on love, which is the bond of perfection.*
- ♦ James 4:6: *But He gives more grace. Therefore He says: "God resists the proud, but gives grace to the humble."*
- ♦ Luke 14:11: *For all those who exalt themselves will be humbled, and those who humble themselves well be exalted.*
- ♦ Proverbs 15:33: *Wisdom's instruction is to fear the Lord, and humility comes before honor.*

Application:

Philadelphia represents a Church that heralds the adage, "They will know we are Christians by our love, by our love, yes, they'll know we are Christians by our love." Most of you reading this will likely have a tune ring out in your head. Though the Church may have been small, they were diligent in their stance with the Lord in word and in deed.

Furthermore, they knew their identities in Christ. They did not allow others to take their crowns. In other words, they understood their value in Christ individually and used it to bless and love the corporate body.

Such a stance is a powerful expression in the body of Christ. When Peter recognized Jesus as the Messiah, all heaven broke loose, Matthew 16:16! There, in front of the gates of hell in Caesarea Philippi, the recognition the world had been waiting for was released. Jesus' life completely shifted once that recognition and declaration was made. No longer did He hang out and minister in the hills of Galilee; now, His eyes turned to Jerusalem. Transfiguration followed, and the road to Jerusalem opened.

Such is the power of acknowledging the gifts and callings of people. By recognizing these gifts, we validate God at work in other's lives, for the gifts and calling of God are irrevocable. More sobering, if we come against someone's calling or are critical and gossip, we may very well be coming up against the living God. That is why gossip is such a sin (2 Corinthians 12:20, Exodus 23:1; James 4:11)! Stealing and denying gifts only leads to demonic division, jealousy, and strife. Thus, the honoring of giftings within the Church at Philadelphia made it a thriving, faultless Church. Even though small and weak by human standards, God's favor was upon them.

Today, God is regenerating the strength of the remnant. He is interested in the integrity and mutual benefits of His gifts and callings within the body, and that they be worked out in love. Thus, in many ways *the new big is small.* When the "small" understand the message of the Church of Philadelphia, its influence will be significant. Why? Because they have entered the irrevocable call of God.

THE CHURCH AT LAODICEA: THE LUKEWARM CHURCH

Founded in the third century BC, Laodicea was located on an important commercial trade route and had become quite prosperous. It had grown so wealthy that when an earthquake partially destroyed it in AD 61, they refused Roman assistance to rebuild. The city was known for its much-desired black wool, banking and as a medical center. It was renowned for its "Phrygian eye-salve": muddy water, that would cure inflammation.

Laodicea had no water supply of its own, and consequently, it was transported in from hot springs in nearby Heiropolis by an aqueduct. Cold waters from the mountain springs also flowed into it from Colossae. By the time it reached its destination, the water had turned lukewarm. Thus, Jesus' letter addressed issues everyone could relate to at the time of the writing. Sewell notes, "Its name designates it as a

Church of mob rule, the democratic church, in which everything was swayed and decided by popular opinion."[21]

Laodicea was a Church where Jesus presents Himself as the true and faithful witness. In other words, He was speaking Truth. As the all-knowing God, He knew their history and had this to say about them, *"I know your works, that you are neither cold nor hot. I could wish you were cold or hot., so then, because you are lukewarm, and neither cold nor hot, I will vomit you out of My mouth"* (Revelation 3:15-16).

Knowing Jesus as Savior is different than knowing Jesus as Lord. In this community, they may have known Him as Savior but not as Lord. The Church may have had a good beginning in Christ but gradually fell away from following Him as they became enamored in the works of men.

As a wealthy financial center, Jesus informed them they did not know the depth of their poverty. He counseled them to buy from Him gold refined by fire and white garments (they produced black garments) that they might become rich through spiritual life and vitality. The gold to which He referred was not the kind used for purchases, but rather the fiery refinement of spiritual lives. Spiritual gold is described by Peter:

> *In this you greatly rejoice, though now for a little while, if need be, you have been grieved by various trials, that the genuineness of your faith, being much more precious than gold that perishes, though it is tested by fire, may be found to praise, honor, and glory at the revelation of Jesus Christ* (1 Peter 1:6-7).

New garments, like any new clothes we buy, are transformative. They change our looks and spiritually represent a sanctified life. Jesus' invitation was to fight the fight of faith: No matter the cost, He exhorts them to lay down earthly comforts, obey and follow the Lord. Though they produced it, they needed the kind of "eye-salve" that would open their blind spiritual eyes to what concerned Him. Jesus was using language they could understand.

In the longest of the letters to the seven churches, Jesus sent strong exhortations to the Laodiceans. He let them know He loved them but cautioned them to be zealous in following Him. He was knocking at their door and wanted to come in to dine with them: *"Behold, I stand at the door and knock, if anyone hears My voice and opens the door I will come in to him and dine with him, and he with Me"* (Revelation 3:20). Dining with someone is an invitation to conversation and intimacy while we nourish our physical bodies. Jesus was offering the opportunity for them to meet with them to be filled with both physical and spiritual nourishment. For those who would overcome their lukewarmness and wholeheartedly follow, He would grant them to "sit with Me on My throne" (v. 20). In other words, they would rule with Christ who held all truth and represented the true God.

Summary of the Church of Laodicea
- ♦ Affirmation:
  - o None.
- ♦ Accusation:
  - o They were lukewarm.
  - o They were blind, poor, and naked, and did not know it.
- ♦ Assurance:
  - o Buy from Jesus gold refined in fire, or faith fueled through fire (1 Peter 1:7).
  - o Wear white garments and have salve for their eyes.
  - o Be zealous and repent. To him who overcomes, Jesus would grant the right to sit with Him on His throne.

Scriptures
- ♦ Isaiah 55:1: *Ho! Everyone who thirsts, come to the waters; and you who have no money, come buy and eat. Yes, come, buy wine and milk without money and without price.*

- Ephesians 4:14-16: *That we should no longer be children, tossed to and fro and carried about with every wind of doctrine, by the trickery of men, in the cunning craftiness of deceitful plotting, but, speaking the truth in love, may grow up in all things into Him who is the head—Christ— from whom the whole body, joined and knit together by what every joint supplies, according to the effective working by which every part does its share, causes growth of the body for the edifying of itself in love.*

- Philippians 3:8-10: *Yet indeed I also count all things loss for the excellence of the knowledge of Christ Jesus my Lord, for whom I have suffered the loss of all things, and count them as rubbish, that I may gain Christ and be found in Him, not having my own righteousness, which is from the law, but that which is through faith in Christ, the righteousness which is from God by faith; that I may know Him and the power of His resurrection, and the fellowship of His sufferings, being conformed to His death.*

- Philippians 3:12: *Not that I have already attained, or am already perfected; but I press on, that I may lay hold of that for which Christ Jesus has also laid hold of me.*

- Matthew 26:41: *Keep watching and praying that you may not enter into temptation; the spirit is willing, but the flesh is weak.*

Application:

Last, but not least, of the churches is Laodicea. The message to this church is clear. Though they had received the Word of God, they were slack in applying it to their lives. Today, the message of the Laodicean Church relays a pre-eminent concern where distractions, busyness, prosperity, entertainment, and all kinds of plans and conspiracies can dangerously put in peril our spiritual lives thrusting us into murky lukewarm waters where it is difficult to see and hear.

We see this repeatedly, particularly in prayer meetings where the initial response is strong, but the spiritual muscle is not developed enough to keep an ongoing effort in place. By and large, the ongoing effort is sustained by the remnant of the faithful. It is this remnant who press on beyond the distractions to place the "one thing," first, as a priority: *"One thing I have desired of the Lord, that will I seek: That I may dwell in the house of the Lord all the days of my life, to behold the beauty of the Lord and to inquire in His temple"* (Psalm 27:4).

When the "one thing" becomes pre-eminent, the lethargy, and Laodicean spirit gives way. Joy breaks forth and through it, new strength. David goes on to say, *"And now my head shall be lifted up above my enemies all around me: Therefore, I will offer sacrifices of joy in His tabernacle; I will sing, yes, I will sing praises to the Lord"* (Psalm 27:6). Such is the reward of those who diligently seek Him.

SUMMARY:

The letters to the seven churches of Revelation are a backbone and a guide for the Body of Christ today in its pursuit of relationship with God and with each other. The letters to the Ephesians and to Laodicea act as bookends to the narrative Jesus relayed to the Church then and for the future. The Ephesians maintained good works, but with detached hearts. Their love had grown cold. The Laodiceans were mired in self-sufficiency and blind to their true spiritual condition.

In between, the letters describe a journey of the heart. In two of the congregations, there are no words of accusation, the Church at Smyrna, and Philadelphia. Smyrna represents the church that overcomes persecution, and the Philadelphia church is described as humble and reliant on God.

However, in two others there was no approval, Sardis and Laodicea. Instead, Jesus declares that He knew their deeds/works but found them lacking. They had become complacent and self-reliant while living on reputation. These accusations were not external problems; the issues were internal—and a warning.

The messages continue to be relevant today for us all to heed. Both the positive and the negative characteristics in these letters offer lessons to sharpen and grow our spiritual muscle. Throughout the missives, consistently, Jesus' words and exhortations were two-fold:

1. *He who has an ear, let him hear what the Spirit says to the churches*: Revelation 2:7, 11, 17, 29; Revelation 3:6, 13, 22
2. *He who overcomes:* Revelation 2:7, 11, 17, 26; Revelation 3:5, 12, 21

In other words, those who overcome the character challenges presented in five of the churches, and apply the good qualities, will reap the rewards and benefits of His Kingdom where genuine gold and spiritual wealth is found. Paul writes of the Lord's promise, *"My grace is sufficient for you, for My strength is made perfect in weakness"* (2 Corinthians 12:7). May it be unto us according to your Word.

But from there you will seek the LORD your God, and you will find Him if you seek Him with all your heart and with all your soul. When you are in distress, and all these things come upon you in the latter days, when you turn to the LORD your God and obey His voice (for the LORD your God is a merciful God),
He will not forsake you nor destroy you,
nor forget the covenant of your fathers which He swore to them.
Deuteronomy 4:29-31

DISCUSSION QUESTIONS:

1. Of the seven churches examined in this chapter, what evidence of each church are you experiencing around you?
2. Discuss "Affirmations" and "Accusations" of the churches. Which ones you can you relate to? How can we position ourselves as believers to be overcomers?

PRAYER POINTS:

The enemy will often attack our weaknesses as well as our strengths. Pray for and affirm each other's strengths and speak life into weaknesses.

ACTION STEPS:

Find scriptures that apply to both your strengths and your weaknesses. Meditate on them and commit to memory. They will divide your soul and spirit when attacks come and help you move into an overcoming spirit that produces the fruit of the Spirit which is love, joy, peace, patience, kindness, goodness and self-control, Galatians 5:22-23.

6

THE REVITALIZATION: THE CORPORATE CALL TO PRAYER

*And let us consider one another in order to stir up love and good
works, not forsaking the assembling of ourselves together, as is the
manner of some, but exhorting one another,
and so much the more as you see the Day approaching.*
Hebrews 10:24-25

A s our culture becomes increasingly resistant to Christian
values, it may be the very catalyst needed to turn the Church
back to Isaiah's mandate to be a "house of prayer for all nations" (Isaiah
56:7). In fact, those who are in so-called "closed nations" that are
resistant to the Gospel have commented they do not want the present-
day pressures against the Church removed, as it would fuel
complacency. God often uses adversities to make His Kingdom known.
We are in times when Jesus is calling forth a pure and spotless bride.
Much of the purification process will be done under the pressures of the
resistance now rising in the nations.

As times intensify, God is moving to restore and revitalize
communities of prayer to the Body of Christ. We are seeing a new
hunger rise in traditional churches and in the prayer movement paving
the way for the Church to enter into more significant corporate
agreement and intimacy with the Lord. In his commentary on Acts, Stott

relays a balanced approach where, with patient endurance, the heart of the Church can change:

> "The Holy Spirit's way with the institutional church, which we long to see reformed according to the gospel, is more the way of patient reform than of impatient rejection. And certainly, it is always healthy when the more formal and dignified services of the local church are complemented with the informality and exuberance of home meetings. There is no need to polarize between the structured and the unstructured, the traditional and the spontaneous. The church needs both."[1]

There will be an ever-increasing challenge and need to train and teach Church leadership on the importance of corporate prayer; and equip leaders with tools to facilitate it. Without vision or leadership, people will perish, Proverbs 29:18. So, how do we build community in prayer? What practical steps can we take to cultivate our local arenas of influence to inspire corporate prayer? Key concepts to facilitate igniting, building, and sustaining healthy communities of contending prayer is the focus of this chapter.

COMMUNITY IN PRAYER IS RISING OUTSIDE THE WALLS OF THE MAINLINE CHURCH:

In working with prayer ministries and groups throughout Europe, Asia, and the South Pacific, we observe God igniting corporate prayer. Much of it occurs outside the established church.

Corporate prayer is happening in what many call the "Prayer Movement." This term is a collective title applying to houses of prayer, prayer ministries, or prayer groups that abound primarily outside the formal Church walls. Though statistics point to significant sidelining of corporate prayer in the traditional church, a growing movement of 24/7 prayer, houses of prayer, and prayer ministries that have emerged over the past several decades must be noted. Much of this movement, by observation, is outside the traditional church walls. Banks notes:

> "Interest in praying together is on the rise. Movements like the 24/7 prayer effort are springing up in Britain, the United States, Australia, and South Africa, based on a centuries-old practice of praying around the clock. There is a growing hunger to see what God alone can do above and beyond our ability to plan or program."[2]

In May of 1999, the International House of Prayer in Kansas City was birthed through the leadership of Mike Bickle and a team of twenty full-time prayer missionaries.[3] They had cried out for thirteen hours a day from May 7, 1999, until September 19, 1999, when they launched 24/7 schedule of prayer that has been non-stop ever since.[4]

Similarly, other 24/7 prayer movements emerged simultaneously through the calling of Dick Eastman, "Every home for Christ," and Peter Grieg, 24/7 Europe.[5] The movement is burgeoning with prayer rooms and houses of prayer across Europe. Though no research on the character and nature of these entities has been done, it is noteworthy that a roster of these rooms exists with a list of over 500 worldwide.[6] It must be mentioned that a plethora of such expressions exist and to date would be a formidable task to count. This roster is not conclusive or exhaustive.

However, in visiting a number of these houses of prayer in different nations, there is frequently sparse participation outside larger corporate centers like IHOPKC. To quantify this type of prayer movement would be difficult. Suffice it to say, that much of it exists peripheral to the present-day typical local church expression.

A study conducted by U.S. News and Beliefnet substantiates this observation. Data was collected regarding prayer practices amongst Christians, Jews, and Muslims. The results indicated that only 4.4% of Christians chose to pray at a house of worship, i.e., formal Church. 79.5% pray in their homes.[7] It would seem apparent these statistics do point to a significant lack of prayer in community in the established Church.

If God is igniting and fueling prayer outside traditional churches, what practical steps can we take to move things forward, towards God's design for His House to be a House of Prayer, and bring the vision inside the local church? In leading people towards intimacy with God, it is key to assess the corporate expression, and whether they are ready and willing to make the deep changes necessary to bring such vision to pass.

Ronald Heifetz emphasizes in his book on leadership, "Start where people are at."[8] He goes on to say, "In managing corporate dynamics, pull back to gain perspective, listen to where people are at, understand authority figures, pastors, and discern what kind of environment is necessary for people to receive it."[9]

Below are six steps in how to influence a church community for those called to this kind of ministry:

1. Develop a personal lifestyle of prayer.
2. Secure your vision.
3. Build relationships.
4. Commit to the task.
5. Honor authority.
6. Build team leadership.

1. DEVELOP A PERSONAL LIFESTYLE OF PRAYER:

If you have a heart to see corporate prayer develop in your local community, the first and most obvious step is to develop your personal prayer life. The book *Could you not Tarry one Hour?* by Larry Lea, greatly impacted our prayer life and personal journey. The book describes a simple way of getting your brain and heart to agree with prayer in three stages. Lea explains:

> "I want to make you a promise: Something supernatural happens when you pray an hour a day. It does not happen

---

overnight, but slowly, almost imperceptibly, the ***desire*** to pray becomes firmly planted in the soil of your heart by the Spirit of God. This desire crowds out the weeds of apathy and neglect, and matures into the ***discipline*** to pray. Then one day you discover that prayer is no longer just a duty or drudgery; instead, the discipline of prayer has borne the fruit of ***delight***. You find yourself eagerly longing for your daily time with God."[10]

Developing friendships takes time. It requires us to make an effort. The same is true with our relationship with God. I read a bumper sticker once, "If God seems far away, it's not because He has moved!" That is a lot of truth in a few words. Spiritual hunger is a driving force to birth desire for intimacy with God. Henri Nouwen articulates the need to make our internal home a place for God to abide:

"Home is the center of my being where I can hear the voice that says: 'You are my Beloved, on you my favor rests'— the same voice that gave life to the first Adam and spoke to Jesus, the second Adam; the same voice that speaks to all the children of God and sets them free to live in the midst of a dark world while remaining in the light. I have heard that voice."[11]

Prayer and worship can't be cooked up in the flesh. It is nurtured by the Holy Spirit and is the vehicle by which intimacy is cultivated.

God will be there if we take the time be with Him. Training our attention to focus on Him through worship and meditating on His Word builds our spiritual muscles. His Word carries significant transformational weight when used and integrated into our lives. When praying His Words over your circumstances, pray in faith, expecting Jesus, your friend, to answer. Take these for a few samples:

- *In the beginning was the Word and the Word with God, and the Word was God* (John 1:1).
- *Your word is truth* (John 17:17).

- *Your word is a lamp to my feet and a light to my path* (Psalm 119:105).
- *"So shall My word be that goes forth from My mouth; It shall not return to Me void, But it shall accomplish what I please, and it shall prosper in the thing for which I sent it,"* (Isaiah 55:11).
- *For the word of the Lord is right and all His work is done in truth* (Psalm 33:4).
- *Therefore whoever hears these sayings of Mine, and does them, I will liken him to a wise man who built his house on the rock* (Matthew 7:24).
- *Your word has given me life* (Psalm 119:50).

When you are struggling with push-back or negativity in your life, own the fact that "Your Word has given me life." Pray it, and believe it, for the concerns that weigh on your heart! By focusing on His Word and worship, we begin to speak life to ourselves, and our challenges become places of victory. Our view of God transforms as we work His Word through our prayers. Our head, our thinking, gets a good dose of His goodness, and suddenly the problems disappear, and the promises of God bring solutions into view. The revelation of the majesty of God becomes a reality. His Words become our words, and a spiritual friendship, and desire follow. That is a divine interchange that builds up spiritual muscle and develops longing to be with Him. Jesus expresses His desire for a relationship with us: *"No longer do I call you servants, but I call you friends"* (John 15:15).

For me, the ultimate test of whether I am walking out this level of engagement with the Lord is answering the question, "Where are my thoughts, particularly when challenged? Are they focused on the problem or on the promises of God?" This question is critical to ask ourselves as God works His nature in us.

Paul cautions, *If then you were raised with Christ, seek those things which are above, where Christ is, sitting at the right hand of God. Set your mind on things above, not on things on the earth* (Colossians 3:2).

97

As we choose to reset our dials and focus on Him, we exercise spiritual maturity. It can feel painful at first, like any new exercise for weak muscles, but eventually it feels right and good. As we discipline ourselves, it becomes a desire that we just can't live without, and the delight of the Lord becomes our strength.

2. SECURE YOUR VISION:

God promises that if we seek Him, we will find Him (Deuteronomy 4:29). From that place of intimacy, the Lord will guide and direct your path. God will ignite your heart with a passion for pursuing that to which He has called you. He is faithful and is watching over His Word to perform it, and it will not return to Him void. The process of seeking Him for direction is vital in days when distractions and concerns for the hour beg our attention.

King Solomon, known for his wisdom, wrote, *Where there is no vision, the people perish* (Proverbs 29:18 KJV). Vision from the Lord is powerful, and when pursued, unlocks the resources of heaven. Participating in God's plan will inspire and ignite your Spirit in a fresh way. Frequently, it will be beyond what you can do on your own and will require faith to pursue it.

Vision can be tried in the fire to test your resolve. However, God is faithful to His Word and will always bring the confirmation needed to move forward. We have often found that it is darkest just before the breakthrough. God allows these moments of doubt and unbelief to strengthen our faith and resolve. He may also test you to remove selfish ambition, pride, jealousy, fear of rejection to prepare your character for the call. In other words, motivation of visionary purpose from God can only endure if it is cultivated from the reality of Jesus working through you. His Words will then be a "lamp to your feet and a light to your path" (Psalm 119:105).

Habakkuk also warns that there may be a delay in the fruition of your vision. *Write the vision make it plain that they may run with it who read it. For the vision is yet for an appointed time. But at the end it will*

98

speak, and it will not lie (Habakkuk 2:2). The Bible is replete with stories of the suddenlies counter-balanced by seasons of waiting. Vision involves both birthing and building. The sudden appearance of an angel to a young virgin announcing the arrival of a Savior broke four hundred years of silence (Luke 1:26-38). In the waiting, God made Mary ready to receive the vision—and the time was right.

Abraham was in his seventies when God first appeared to him, but it was twenty-five-plus years later before the promise of Isaac came to fruition, Genesis 17:17. Sarah was ninety and Abraham 100! Long seasons of waiting may prepare the way for a "set time" when God performs His Word. It becomes an "only God can do this" moment, and He is glorified. So do not despise the days of small beginnings, nor seasons of waiting in seemingly unfruitful places; rather, continue to worship and seek the Lord. Develop your gifting to serve the Body of Christ and watch to see what will happen.

3. BUILD RELATIONSHIPS:

In days of increasing lawlessness, God is turning hearts back to the basic foundations of our faith. When questioned by the Pharisees as to what the great commandment in the law was, Jesus responded:

> "*You shall love the LORD your God with all your heart, with all your soul, and with all your mind. This is the first and great commandment. And the second is like it: You shall love your neighbor as yourself. On these two commandments hang all the Law and the Prophets*" (Matthew 22:37-40).

The antidote to the alienation and division experienced by so many in the Church lies in relationship. Many like to quote Jesus' words, "*Again I say to you that if two of you agree on earth concerning anything that they ask, it will be done for them by My Father in heaven. For where two or three are gathered together in My name, I am there in the midst*

—

of them" (Matthew 18:19). However, it must be noted that the previous four verses (v.15-19) all deal with keeping our relationships healthy.

The enemy hates corporate prayer because of its potential to catalyze the Church into action and take territory previously held in his grip. Laying solid foundations of relationship with those building into a community of prayer is vital for its future and health.

The quality of your community will significantly impact the effectiveness of your prayers. Peter Grieg and David Blackwell of 24/7 Europe state, "In our experience, the biggest factor in making 24/7 work for a sustained period of time, is not the size of the group, but the strength of the community."[12] Agreement is everything in corporate prayer. When we touch the heart of God in personal prayer, the impact is transformative.

However, the cross is horizontal as well as vertical. The quality of our community will, in many ways, impact the effectiveness of our prayers. Luke describes the Acts church as being in *one accord* repeatedly, Acts 1:14; 2:1, 46; 4:24; 5:12; 7:57; 8:6; 12:20; 15:25. The word accord or *homothymadon*, means unanimously with one mind. This level of agreement within the early Church caused an explosive dynamic to erupt on earth, catapulting the Gospel into the nations with transformative force. As we face insurmountable challenges today, we need this kind of power of God to work through His Church.

When starting a corporate prayer expression, stick with those who are hungry and show a desire. Develop a relationship with them and commit to meet. Numbers are not the measure of success. Your relationship with God, one another, and consistency in regularly gathering are the decisive metrics.

The ***new big is small.*** When God decides to do something, He will often choose a remnant. Work with those God has given you. Develop them and bring them to a place of intimacy and breakthrough where "Only God" experiences can explain His working in your midst. As He is glorified; we are strengthened, the testimony grows, and His Spirit propels everyone along.

Hospitality is essential when building a sense of community. The coffee shops of the world are great conversation hang-outs. And don't forget to have fun! Laughter is a great medicine that can forge strong and lasting bonds. Effective communities of contending prayer will have foundations of relational strength. Such foundations generate safe environments where people can feel free to worship and pray.

Daniel and three dedicated Hebrews set up their community of contending prayer in the heart of resistant Babylon. What happened between them changed history. Their combined dedication yielded spiritual breakthrough, favor and influence in a resistant government. Jesus chose twelve untrained, unskilled men and changed the world. Countless times in the Bible, God uses a remnant for His purposes. Remnants committed to God and one another are powerful Kingdom collaborators in His hands.

4. COMMIT TO MEET:

Commitment is vital in developing the willingness and readiness to surrender to God. Ruth Barton emphasizes this precondition to joining in what God is doing, "It does no good to discern the will of God if we are not committed to doing it."[13] Psalm 37:5 states, *Commit your way to the Lord, trust also in Him, and He shall bring it to pass.*

In this verse, the word translated as "commit" is the Hebrew word "gâlal" meaning to "to roll over" or "roll away."[14] It is the same word that is used when Jacob "rolled away" the stone from the well to allow Laban's sheep to come and drink, Genesis 29:3. How do you put those two meanings together? It can connote the effort required to "roll away" one's troubles over to someone who can help. When we are in trouble, who do we turn to for help? Galal takes us from handling our difficulties ourselves to committing to the Lord to see us through. A New Testament expression of this commitment is found in Peter's words exhorting us to resist the enemy by, "Casting all your care upon Him, for He cares for you" (1 Peter 5:6).

This story of "galal," committing our ways to the Lord, is a picture for us today of the power of faithfulness in prayer. Committing to and contending in corporate prayer breaks open a spiritual well to drink from God's Presence. The doors of His covenant plan will then unfold. Our faithful commitment to the Lord will fuel the thirst for more, and we "run the race with endurance so as to win the prize" (1 Corinthians 9:24). As we commit, God sees our integrity and trust builds. Psalm 41:12 relays, *As for me, You uphold me in my integrity, and set me before Your face forever.*

As a word of caution, set reasonable goals. Don't bite off more than you can chew. In other words, when starting something, you will want to strategize for the long haul. Answering a few key questions will help you formulate a plan going forward:

1. What is your group's focus?
2. Is the group forming for your local church body, city, region/state, nation?
3. What is the level of spiritual maturity, commitment and interest in those who would participate?

It is important for your prayer community to identify its purpose. History is replete with stories of how a small, insignificant group resolute in purpose and prayer moved the heart of God. From the two elderly women in Scotland's Hebrides revival, to Herrnhut, Germany, to the Haystack revival in Williamstown, Massachusetts—to name only a few—small, committed, contending prayer groups, with sincere and contrite hearts, apprehended God's heart; and earth shattering, history-making moves of Spiritual renewal resulted. Our previous examples show that the contending remnant of believers change history through prayer and agreement. Commitment leads the way for others to witness a sincerity that opens the pathway for others to follow.

5. HONOR AUTHORITY:

As stated, much of the mainline Church today does not understand or engage in "corporate prayer." If you are one of those with a passion to see corporate prayer/worship re-established in your congregation, know it is God raising this desire.

Frequently, those called will not necessarily be the pastors. Jesus is zealous for His Church. The tables are turning and yes, Jesus is surely more passionate than us for His house to be a house of prayer for all nations. We need to trust our Lord for His Church. It is not our responsibility. Our charge is to respond to His call.

As corporate prayer is not a priority in the present-day, average church, don't expect to receive a lot of understanding responses when first stepping out. Rather, express honor for those in leadership as you develop relationship. Know whose roof you are under and act accordingly. Pray for an opening in which you are invited to express your vision. Work with the local leadership within your church or community and investigate where other groups may have formed, or leaders called and find out their vision or purpose. Seek ways to develop relationship and potential for collaboration that honor the various callings. Relational strength is key for any further future efforts and growth.

As a pastor, Lawler gives sound advice in developing corporate prayer within a local church body, "Consider talking to your pastor about prayer in the body. Be respectful and patient. My goal is not to breed crazed prayer terriers nipping at pastoral heels. Don't talk to your pastor *about* prayer unless you are already talking to God *for* your pastor. Please reread the preceding sentences (in this quote) two more times!"[15]

Once you understand and get a feel for the dynamics of the local leadership, you can begin developing the necessary relationship to express your vision and calling. Inevitably, in developing corporate prayer, problems will arise from two main issues: first, when relationships have not been properly formed; or second, when authority has not been honored. You will be saved from the heartaches of people misunderstanding and misrepresenting your good intentions by paying attention to these two vital facets of corporate health.

6, BUILD TEAM LEADERSHIP:

As Jesus is our ultimate example, His life and leadership modeled team dynamics. His team started when He chose the most unlikely of men to follow Him. Somehow, He saw beyond the natural into the potential of each of His future disciples. He chose the weak and foolish things that would someday "shame the wise" 1 Corinthians 1:27.

Those drawn to corporate prayer may also be of this understated nature. We cannot bypass anyone in the call to corporate prayer. In his book on leadership, Arthur Boers states, "God's most important work does not necessarily occur through the high and mighty, the strong and the powerful. God acts, rather, through unlikely and unknown, out-of-the-way fringe folks."[16]

How each of the disciples began their journey with Jesus certainly differed by the end of their time with Him on earth. His influence transformed each of them. Boers points out, "While we may identify leadership with prestige and elite standing, the Bible generally commends leadership as a way to pursue justice. This point of view is communicated by the frequent selection of unattractive and unlikely leaders. Time after time, they had no obvious leadership qualities and came from out-of-the-way places—in other words people who would not necessarily stand out as seminary 'stars.'"[17]

Luke records in Acts, *Now when they saw the boldness of Peter and John, and perceived that they were uneducated and untrained men, they marveled. And they realized that they had been with Jesus* (Acts 4:13). The boldness of the disciples reflected their "followership" with Jesus. God is a transformational God. He is searching for the willing vessels— those that He can shape. As the disciples were bold, they exhibited how vision and energy are important in a team. John Maxwell, in his book on team leadership notes, "The people on a team will sacrifice and work together only if they can see what they're working toward."[18]

In three short years, Jesus poured into these men the nature of God and signs followed. His teachings and demonstrations of power changed their lives. Jesus formed His team, then devoted His time to discipling them. He lived out team leadership by what He taught them. They learned patience in the parable of the fig tree, Luke 13:6-9. He inspired faith when they had little faith. He called out to Peter who walked on water: *And immediately Jesus stretched out His hand and caught him, and said to him, "O you of little faith, why did you doubt?" And when they got into the boat, the wind ceased* (Matthew 14:31-32). These are only a sample of all that transpired between them. But during His short three years of mentorship, Jesus laid the foundations of apostolic team ministry.

When developing corporate prayer, lead as Jesus did by looking into the value of people. They may seem the most unlikely yet show the interest. Drawing the best out of people is the kind of team leadership Jesus always modeled and He is the one we should emulate.

Ed Silvoso describes a 5-15-80 percent principle in developing your community, your team. He gave this breakdown: 5% of the people will be *visionaries* who see the vision and are immediately on board; 15% are *implementers* who readily grasp the vision and desire to make it happen; 80% are *maintainers* who need to see the impact of the vision before they embrace it.[19] Cultivating and understanding your team in this manner will help you mobilize the forerunners for others to follow.

In his book on leadership, Roger Heuser states, "No matter how it presents itself, the call ascends to occupy the primacy of all of one's desires and goals. For those who hear the call, there is no alternative."[20]

It can take a long season of living a lifestyle of integrity, regularly and persistently "walking out" the talk, for people to notice and show interest in joining a prayer group. You cannot walk the talk of prayer and intimacy without doing it yourself. People eventually catch it when they see you pay and pray the price and witness the testimony from it. Quinn summarizes this well, "By taking a moral position and pursuing what is right for the collective, other organizational members are motivated by the leader's actions and power…Thus when organizational members see their leader 'walking the walk and talking the talk,' they themselves are inspired to take significant risks for the good of the collective."[21]

SUMMARY:

We have often heard in ministry that we need to quantify our success. Is that possible when it is about intimacy with the Lord and corporate prayer? Sure, we have seen God's powerful answers, signs and wonders, but how do you quantify that? Story after story of corporate prayer and worship interventions have led to historic changes for nations. Still, frequently such work is done in small insignificant groups that are relentless in prayer.

Boers corroborates stating, "Worldly leadership prioritizes power and coercion; violence and fear play a large role. Jesus' kingdom is characterized by compassion, hospitality, healing. Furthermore, scriptures show that what the world rates as triumphs are ultimately vain. Victory and success in worldly kingdoms mean conquering, defeating, and eliminating enemies. But in God's kingdom, faithfulness may mean martyrdom (as for John). Suffering is more likely than success. Persecution and misunderstanding are expected. Ministry frequently ends in tragedy. But no matter, as witnessing to God's priorities persists."[22]

Those working in the prayer/worship world risk encountering challenges and the disappointment of being misunderstood and sidelined. However, that is often how God chooses a remnant. What communities of committed prayer accomplish are not well understood today's "numbers"-driven Christian culture. Yet, in these small cells are elements of God's covenant, agreement, relationship, and kingdom realities that shake heaven and earth. Increasingly, the understanding that *the new big is small* is making its way into the framework of church function. God's ways our not man's ways. In the coming storm, these small cells may very well be the herald and lamppost for a church increasingly called to the frontlines of battle.

Commit your way to the Lord,
Trust also in Him,
And He shall bring it to pass.
He shall bring forth your righteousness as the light,
And your justice as the noonday.
Psalm 37:5-6

DISCUSSION QUESTIONS:

1. The new big is small. Of the six steps in developing corporate prayer, which ones do you feel confident about, and which ones require more work? Discuss what you can do about it.
2. What are some practical actions you can take for each of the six mentioned steps?
3. Have you ever embraced/rejected any visions from the Lord due to a particular level of "buy in" from those around you?
4. If there is no present expression of corporate prayer in your church community, what practical steps can you take to initiate such a vision? And to build agreement towards it?

PRAYER POINTS:

1. Pray for those in authority in your local church to receive and understand the value of the corporate prayer expression for your local community.
2. If you have corporate prayer working in your church, pray for God to multiply and expand the vision to reach children, young adults, men and women, elderly, cultural spheres of society.

\

ACTION STEPS:

1. Given your present local expression of church, what practical steps can you take to promote corporate prayer in your community?
   a. To initiate a corporate prayer expression
   b. Or to participate in corporate prayer

7

THE RE-ENGAGED: PRAYER AND ACTION

"As you have sent Me into the world,
I also have sent them into the world."
John 17:18

By Dr. Frederic Rowe

W e are in times when faith, prayer and action are being called to the front lines. God is calling the Church out of its four walls. It has been said, "If you doubt the power of prayer, consult your history books."[1] True to the statement, history books are lined with the testimony of Jesus moving on behalf of the prayers of His people. Whatever the testimony, God's profound love for us, and His creation is relayed through the stories: some are written on the pages of books, and some written on the tablets of our hearts. All of them unite prayer and inspire action. As for prayer, Banks notes: "Prayer not only should precede action, it is action of the highest kind because it gives God the priority He deserves."[2] In this paradigm, prayer itself becomes the initiator of the action that follows.

When Jesus came, He exhibited a lifestyle of both prayer and action. His presence and ministry disrupted the culture. He was sent to the earth not to be separated from it, but to engage with it and be an example for us. John relays Jesus' words, *"As you have sent Me into the world, I also have sent them into the world"* (John 17:18). Jesus never meant for His life in us to be isolated. The text further explains, *"I do not pray for these alone, but also for those who will believe in Me through their word"* (John 17:20). If we genuinely want to see the power of God at work, we need to link corporate prayer with action on the issues over which we pray. Robert Mulholland explains in his book on spiritual formation that we have two inseparable dimensions as believers, "One is our life of personal intimacy with God, the other is our life of public intimacy with God. These are neither either-or nor both/and options; they are inseparable."[3] Jesus never intended us to pray and not follow through with some action. Action, motivated by the Holy Spirit, is a clear part of the biblical mandate for us all.

THE BIBLICAL MANDATE FOR PRAYER AND ACTION:

God delegated the authority to man, both men and women, to bring the earth into submission. He gave us everything that we need to fulfill this assignment. The mandate starts in Genesis 1:27-28:

> *God created mankind in His own image, in the image of God he created them; male and female he created them. God blessed them and said to them, "Be fruitful and increase in number; fill the earth and subdue it. Rule over the fish in the sea and the birds in the sky and over every living creature that moves on the ground."*

The word "subdue" is the Hebrew word, kâḇaš, meaning to conquer, subjugate, bring into subjection.[4] God's original intent was for man to "tend and keep the garden" He gave us (Genesis 2:15). But it was contingent upon man's obedience to God. Bill NeSmith reviews and asserts this authority given in Genesis 1:26-28:

> "The first thing to notice from this verse is that the word "over" is used five times in verse 26 and three more times in

verse 28. In this whole section of Scripture, God makes the idea of dominion more evident as He says to be fruitful, to multiply, to replenish the earth, and to subdue it—ultimately having dominion or authority "over every living thing that moveth upon the earth" and to maintain prominence. Man is to be stewards of all creation, being granted dominion over it by the Creator of all things. As God knows the end from the beginning, and He instilled the wild nature in all creation, He told Adam to "subdue" (Hebrew: כָּבַשׁ – kabash – Strong's #3533 – "to subdue, bring into subjection")31 or bring into subjection, subjugate under a proper order of authority. This authority stems from God, flowing through unfallen man, to all creation. In original intent, man had the capability within him to rule righteously as an honorable and benevolent caregiver."[5]

After the fall in the Garden in Genesis 3, man lost his influence to accomplish this responsibility. Throughout the rest of the Old Testament, the story of the Bible relays man's inability to obey God and return to his original assignment without a Savior. The Savior, Jesus, put man back on the right track by delegating His authority to us through His death and resurrection. Matthew 28:18-20, the Great Commission, lays it out for us:

> *Then Jesus came to them and spoke to them saying, "All authority has been given to Me in heaven and on earth. Go therefore and make disciples of all the nations, baptizing them in the name of the Father and of the Son and of the Holy Spirit, teaching them to observe all things that I have commanded you; and lo, I am with you always, even to the end of the age."* *Amen* (Matthew 28:18-20).

There are several things to take note of from this passage. First, man was again given the delegated authority from God. But now, the assignment becomes more specific. It went from "fill the earth and subdue it" to "go and make disciples of all nations." The second point is that the passage does not say, "Go, and make disciples *in* all nations." Rather, it says, "Go, and make disciples *of* all nations." These passages relay the fact that God is not looking only at the individual. He is also looking at the society in which the individual lives.

How do you use your delegated authority from God to disciple a nation, baptizing and teaching obedience to all that Jesus commanded? The only way we can do this is to use our authority to influence and engage with people at every level— not just in religious activities— but in the family, business, government, education, arts and media. In other words, if we are to disciple a nation, we must engage and influence the entire society where we reside.

There is another crucial passage that speaks to the engagement of man with the world around him. Matthew writes:

> *"You are the salt of the earth; but if the salt loses its flavor, how shall it be seasoned? It is then good for nothing but to be thrown out and trampled underfoot by men. You are the light of the world. A city that is set on a hill cannot be hidden. Nor do they light a lamp and put it under a basket, but on a lampstand, and it gives light to all who are in the house. Let your light so shine before men, that they may see your good works and glorify your Father in heaven"* (Matthew 5:13-16).

This passage is part of the Sermon on the Mount. In this teaching, Jesus laid out our identity and purpose. It specifically illustrates that the people of the nations are to see our good works, which are the result of letting our light shine before others. We must not hide our efforts. They must be visible to the people around us and done in such a way that people will see the hand of God in what we are doing to glorify Him, not us.

Such effort is impossible to do without us walking in the power and the presence of God. And that is how prayer is connected to action. To be effective witnesses, people must see God's hand at work in what we do. This visibility means we need to be constantly praying, not just by ourselves, but with others. We must have the mutual power of agreement with God in prayer to fulfill our corporate assignment. Such community is necessary because God's assignment cannot be done on our own strength.

John 15 speaks to the necessity of walking closely with God in everything we do. To do this, we must be walking in His presence or abiding in Him. John exhorts: *"Abide in Me, and I in you. As the branch cannot bear fruit of itself, unless it abides in the vine, neither can you, unless you abide in Me. I am the vine, you are the branches. He who abides in Me, and I in him, bears much fruit; for without Me you can do nothing"* (John 15:4-5).

The key to having good works that will cause others to notice and glorify God is to abide in Him, which means being constantly in His presence. If we do this, God lays out an amazing promise for us: *"If you abide in Me, and My words abide in you, you will ask what you desire, and it shall be done for you. By this My Father is glorified, that you bear much fruit; so you will be My disciples"* (John 15:7-8)

"Abide in me" speaks to prayer; and "bear much fruit" speaks to action. It is not possible to separate the two. And why is corporate prayer so important? It is because when we agree with God and with each other, He moves supernaturally on our behalf. Jesus promises: *"Again I say to you that if two of you agree on earth concerning anything that they ask, it will be done for them by My Father in heaven. For where two or three are gathered together in My name, I am there in the midst of them"* (Matthew 18:19-20). Note that it does not take large numbers of people. Agreement with just two or three activates the hand of God.

These words recorded in Matthew are what Jesus said. We also need to see what Jesus did because He is the primary example of how to "make disciples of all nations." It is impossible to read the Gospels without observing they are filled with stories of Jesus interacting with the people of the nation in which He lived (Israel). He interacted with the rich, the poor, with women, and with children, in addition to men. From all walks of life, He healed the sick and delivered the possessed. He spent time with businessmen, governmental authorities, religious authorities, tax collectors, farmers, shepherds, fishermen and teachers. He crossed cultural divides and fellowshipped with Samaritans. He never avoided the outcasts of society: lepers, prostitutes, beggars. Jesus would occasionally withdraw for brief periods to pray. But then, he would go right back to personally influencing and interacting with everyone with whom he came into contact. His entire ministry was one of prayer and action.

ACTIVISM IN THE CHURCH

History is replete with stories of God's people praying and taking action—changing the course of history. The Battle of the Bulge in World War II is one example of history-making prayer. During the battle, 12,000 men were trapped and besieged at Bastogne, Belgium. They had been trapped by foul weather. No one could move, and supplies were low. General Patton only needed a small window to send in the needed replacements. He gave Third Army Chaplain Colonel James O'Neill the order to write a prayer and send it to the troops. Hundreds of thousands of cards were made with the following prayer:

> "Almighty and most merciful Father, we humbly beseech Thee, of Thy great goodness, to restrain these immoderate rains with which we have had to contend. Grant us fair weather for battle. Graciously hearken to us as soldiers who call upon Thee that, armed with Thy power, we may advance from victory to victory, and crush the oppression and wickedness of our enemies and establish Thy justice among men and nations."[6]

As the army prayed, God answered—and the weather cleared. Patton sent in the troops to reinforce the embattled army in what would become "Patton's finest hour." O'Neill was later awarded a Bronze Star for writing the prayer.[7]

When we talk of discipling a nation, an example is the formation of the United States of America. Many of the core elements of the founding documents came from biblical truths that were preached from the pulpits throughout the colonies. A great example of this is the Reverend John Wise. He was a Pastor in Ipswich, Massachusetts, who preached in the late 1600s concerning the issues of the day. Much of the content from his sermons showed up in the Declaration of Independence almost 100 years later. Excerpts from his teachings include:

- "Taxation without representation is tyranny."
- The "consent of the people" is the foundation of government.
- "Every man must be acknowledged equal to every man."

His works were reprinted in 1772 to remind the citizens in the colonies of the core biblical principles of government.[8]

Not only did the truth from the pulpits get into the day-to-day interactions of the colonists, but many of the influential leaders who helped form the US government were pastors and teachers. In fact, many of the signers of the Declaration of Independence were ministers.

Here is a partial list of seven of the fifty-six signers.

- The Rev. Dr. John Witherspoon was a Pastor who then became President of the College of New Jersey (which is now Princeton) in 1768.
- Robert Treat Paine was a chaplain who later became Attorney General of Massachusetts and justice on the state Supreme Court.
- Lyman Hall was an ordained Congregational Minister who later became Governor of Georgia.
- Francis Hopkinson was a church musician and organist who compiled and edited the first hymnbook produced solely in America.

♦ The Rev. Abraham Baldwin, was a chaplain in the Revolutionary War. He founded the University of Georgia, which had the declared purpose of teaching religion to students. He also served in the first U.S. House of Representatives, where he helped frame the Bill of Rights.

♦ Hugh Williamson was a licensed preacher in the Presbyterian Church. He served in the first U.S. Congress and also helped frame the Bill of Rights.

♦ Roger Sherman was a lay theologian who signed the Constitution in addition to the Declaration of Independence. [9]

These men, and many others like them, were men of both prayer and action. They did not simply pray in the quiet of their homes. They preached the Word of God and through their leadership in government used their gifts to help disciple a nation.

INACTION IN THE WESTERN CHURCH:

Compare the biblical mandate for prayer and action in America's founding fathers compared with the church today. Over the last several decades, the church seems to have been in retreat. Instead of influencing our society, we are complaining about it. Instead of walking out our part of "making disciples of all nations," we have been limiting our ministry to inviting people to church and then outsourcing our responsibilities to pastors. While we sit in the pews, we expect the clergy to share the Gospel, lead people to Christ, baptize new believers, and then disciple them. We have somehow convinced ourselves that all we need to do is go to church on Sunday. We have not been praying. We have not been studying the Bible. And we have not been walking in the power and presence of God. In other words, we have been doing exactly what

Jesus told us not to do, which is to put our light in a basket, where it has little to no effect on those around us.

Even worse, we have avoided whole segments of society because we have been afraid of their negative influence on us. Politics and government, entertainment and arts, media, and higher education are the most prominent examples. We have also complained about the homeless, indignant that the government has not done more to eliminate the problem. We have avoided the poor, seeking to live in places that have safe neighborhoods and good schools. We seem to have forgotten the truth of 1 John 4:4, *"You are of God, little children, and have overcome them, because He who is in you is greater than he who is in the world."*

Instead, we have chosen to withdraw from the world, hoping to avoid evil instead of overcoming it. We have also forgotten that true faith must be demonstrated through our good deeds. James exhorts:

> *"What does it profit, my brethren, if someone says he has faith but does not have works? Can faith save him? If a brother or sister is naked and destitute of daily food, and one of you says to them, 'Depart in peace, be warmed and filled,' but you do not give them the things which are needed for the body, what does it profit? Thus also faith by itself, if it does not have works, is dead"* (James 2:14-17).

We can discuss and argue about how we got here, but the solution; is to get back on once we are clear about how far we have gone off course. Such a turning is the true repentance of which 2 Chronicles 7:14 speaks: *If My people who are called by My name will humble themselves, and pray and seek My face, and turn from their wicked ways, then I will hear from heaven, and will forgive their sin and heal their land.*

THE PATH AHEAD:

The path ahead is calling for the Body of Christ to arise. It is not going to get easier, and our Lord wants us to be strong and of good courage. He who is faithful will not leave or forsake us. He is a covenant-keeping God. Many of the difficulties we are facing, and will face, are to strengthen the Body of Christ. As the governments overreach, and their authority becomes more dictatorial, we see an increase in both prayer and action. For example, in California, when a state of emergency was declared due to COVID 19, in March, 2020, the Governor and his advisors put together a list of what were deemed essential services and businesses that could stay open and continue operation in some form. Churches were not on that list.

Consequently, on March 19, 2020, Californians were told that they could not gather for in-person Church services. This included small group meetings in homes in addition to services in church buildings. Most churches either went online or shut down completely. There were a few exceptions. Harvest Rock Church, in Pasadena, California, was one of them. Led by their Senior Pastor, Che Ahn, the church filed a lawsuit in federal court to stay open. As the case navigated its way through the court system, the parishioners were threatened with criminal prosecution, heavy fines, and even jail time if they continued to meet.[10]

However, the people of Harvest Rock Church would not be intimidated. Knowing their first amendment rights were being violated, they sought out a definitive legal remedy. After several Supreme Court rulings speaking to this matter, the courts finally ruled in their favor, almost a year after they filed the initial lawsuit.

> "On Monday, a California District Court entered an order approving Liberty Counsel's settlement of the lawsuit on behalf of Pasadena's Harvest Rock Church and Harvest International Ministry against the California governor.
>
> Under the settlement, the state of California may no longer impose discriminatory restrictions upon any houses of worship. It's the first statewide permanent injunction in the

country against COVID restrictions on churches and places of worship. The governor must also pay Liberty Counsel $1,350,000 in reimbursement of attorney's fees and costs."[11]

Certainly, many hours of prayer were spent on behalf of the churches in California during this time. Thousands of people were praying. In conjunction with the prayers, the bold actions have served to begin to shift the culture in the direction of greater freedom to worship, which is to the benefit of all; and moves us one step closer to fulfilling the biblical mandate.

SUMMARY:

When we pray corporately, we grow closer to the Lord, particularly when our prayer time includes listening to His voice. It allows Him to share His heart with us. When He does so, it will naturally stir us and motivate us to action. How can it not? This interaction is part of His plan. When God speaks to us, it is not just for good conversation. God is love, and love acts on our behalf.

But it is not just us that God loves. He loves the world and everyone in it. We are His ministers of reconciliation: *Now all things are of God, who has reconciled us to Himself through Jesus Christ, and has given us the ministry of reconciliation, that is, that God was in Christ reconciling the world to Himself, not imputing their trespasses to them, and has committed to us the word of reconciliation* (2 Corinthians 5:18-19). We demonstrate our love for Him by obeying His commands, "If you love Me, keep My commandments" (John 14:15). We walk out our love for Him and others through action. That means we are called to combine our prayers with action by doing our part to fulfill the Great Commission and make disciples of all nations.

DISCUSSION QUESTIONS:

1. Describe what level your current sphere of influence is, i.e.: colleagues, friends and family, community involvement, volunteer, manager, employee.

   a. What cultural sphere do you identify with and how can you influence it for Christ? Arts & Entertainment, Business, Church, Education, Family, Media, Government.[12]

2. In your sphere of influence, what is your biggest challenge or fear in influencing it for Christ? How can you overcome it?

3. On a scale of 1-5, five being greater, how much have you contributed to your sphere of influence through prayer?

4. How does abiding with the Father and corporate prayer alter your influence?

PRAYER POINTS:

1. Pray for boldness
2. Pray for specific strategy to influence your cultural sphere or community for Christ.

ACTION STEPS:

1. Step out and encourage someone today. Make an extra effort to intentionally complement someone daily until it becomes a habit to draw out the best in people around you.

8

THE REDEEMED: GOD IS LOVE

For I am persuaded that neither death nor life,
nor angels nor principalities nor powers,
nor things present nor things to come, nor height nor depth,
nor any other created thing,
shall be able to separate us from the love of God
which is in Christ Jesus our Lord.
Romans 8:38-39

In a book focused on restoring God's house of prayer, it would be remiss not to mention the importance of knowing Him as the author and creator of life itself. Individual lives and our spiritual health matter to the Lord. Our understanding and receiving His love has everything to do with life and health. Love is created in and through Him, for He is love. Knowing and receiving His adoption as a good Father is foundational for our well-being.

From the Garden of Eden to now, the enemy has tried to separate us from His love and life to make us feel orphaned, abandoned, unworthy, insecure, hopeless and disconnected. All of us will experience rejection to one degree or another. The accuser will accuse us of our weaknesses and failures to separate us from the extended hand of a Father who loves to redeem and restore.

God so longs for this relationship with us that He sent His only begotten Son to bridge the gap of separation. After the fall, God first stepped out in search of Adam and Eve in the Garden. *And they heard the sound of the LORD God walking in the garden in the cool of the day, and Adam and his wife hid themselves from the presence of the LORD God among the trees of the garden* (Genesis 3:8). He knew what had happened. The Hebrew word for *walking* is the word *hâlak̄*. Strong's describes this word as continually, to be conversant, exercise, follow.[1] In other words, the walk was intentional. It does not describe a relaxing, meandering walk in the park. There was purpose and engagement in the gait. As Adam and Eve hid, God was already working His plan of redemption.

Do we know and receive His outstretched hand and love in a Spirit of adoption in our personal lives? Every Christian will be tested in this way. Why? That we may know and understand His love.

THE CHOICE:

When we approach God, we have two choices. We can do so as slaves in bondage, or we can approach Him as adopted children. The spirit of slavery is prevalent throughout the Bible, as it wars against God's chosen and His redemptive plan. From Satan tempting Adam and Eve in the Garden, to the conflict between Isaac and Ishmael, David and Saul, to the end-time battles of Daniel 11, Ezekiel 38-39, Revelation, the spirit of slavery has worked to steal, kill and destroy our inheritance in Christ.

However, throughout God's redemptive history, He has raised deliverers, heroes, and heroines, who know the war cry of "Abba Father;" who respond in the Spirit of adoption and resist the enemy's taunts to threaten them, kill or push them aside. The nature of adoption is imperative to understand for our personal and corporate spiritual health and vitality. John expresses God's desire for intimacy with Him:

> *"No longer do I call you servants, for a servant does not know what his master is doing; but I have called you friends, for all things that I heard from My Father I have made known to you.*

You did not choose Me, but I chose you and appointed you that you should go and bear fruit, and that your fruit should remain, that whatever you ask the Father in My name He may give you. These things I command you, that you love one another" (John 15:15-17).

So, how do we know if we are working through a Spirit of adoption? Why is it important? We are living in days when God's Word is being highly contested, and we must be ready to stand up for His righteousness and justice in days of increasing opposition and rejection.

Some reading this may have been so crushed by harsh treatment that it is hard even to read these words and receive the revelation of God as a loving Father and as a trusted friend. The purpose of this chapter is to remove the stumbling blocks, the stones in our hearts, so that we can apprehend Him in the fullness for which He created us. Without the removal of these stones, we cannot see to receive what He is doing.

We are living in the time of which Jesus spoke, *"Most assuredly, I say to you, he who believes in Me, the works that I do he will do also; and greater works than these he will do, because I go to the Father,"* (John 14:12). The Spirit of adoption will guide us into these greater works. Understanding adoption is vital if we are to make our hearts His home, prepared for the greater works and readied to receive the harvest. We receive this Spirit and make our hearts His home by abiding in His Presence and His Word. God is a covenant-keeping God. Ethan the Ezrahite records the power and stability of God's covenant in Psalm 89:34, *My Covenant I will not break nor alter the word that has gone out of My lips.*

God's Word is solid food upon which to feed our souls, (mind, will and emotions), with Truth that fills our spirit with His love. When adoption operates, obedience as sons and daughters shifts from the slave-duty mindset to joyful obedience. So, let's examine the differences between slavery and adoption.

THE ENTRAPMENT OF SLAVERY:

Slavery will keep us in bondage to the rules and regulations of religion and measuring our actions. It will cause us to feel isolated, abandoned, angry and alone. Those entrapped in this mindset will always strive to prove their worth, comparing themselves with others.

One of the most poignant stories of rejection in the Bible was that of Hagar and Ishmael. Through their efforts to have a child and a son of promise, Sarai and Abram made a series of bad decisions. Being barren, Sarai gave Hagar, her servant, to Abram. Ishmael was conceived, and the rancor between Sarai and Hagar began. Trying to escape the harsh treatment, Hagar tried to run, but was sent back to serve Sarai through the promise and counsel of angelic intervention.

Ishmael was born and grew up with Abram as his father and Hagar, his mother. The Lord then appeared to Abram giving him specific instructions on circumcision, Genesis 17:10-14 and changing his name to Abraham, v. 5, and Sarai's name to Sarah (v. 15). Shortly after receiving these instructions from the Lord, Abraham circumcised Ishmael when he was thirteen years old. Abraham was also circumcised at the same time, Genesis 17:25-26. Circumcision was a covenantal act towards God and certainly would have been a bonding moment between father and son.

Soon after this, the time came for Sarah and Abraham to have their long waited-for promise of Isaac. When Isaac was weaned, Abraham made a great feast, Genesis 21:8. Sarah saw Ishmael scoffing and demanded he be cast out of the camp. God spoke to Abraham and counseled him to concede to Sarah's wishes, Genesis 21:12. He sent Hagar and Ishmael out into the Wilderness of Beersheba with a wineskin of water on her shoulder (v.18). Ishmael would have been at least fifteen years old when this happened.

When they ran out of water, Hagar set the boy under a bush and, in desperation, left him there. Departing and going about a "bow shot" away (v.16), in desperate straits, the Lord met her. In her pleading, He opened her eyes to the supply of water nearby, and she filled the skin with water, and they were both able to drink.

In one day, Ishmael lost his father, what he had known as home, almost lost his mother, and never recovered any of his former life again. That is a lot for a fifteen-year-old to handle. The rejection he endured took root and continues to wreak havoc between the descendants of Ishmael—including Mohammed and those now in the grip of Islam; and the sons of Isaac and his son Jacob—the Jewish people today. The author of Hebrews warns us, *Pursue peace with all people, and holiness, without which no one will see the Lord: looking carefully lest anyone fall short of the grace of God; lest any root of bitterness springing up cause trouble, and by this many become defiled* (Hebrews 12:14-15).

Rejection and unforgiveness will greatly cloud our understanding of God. Such roots allow jealousy, anger and bitterness to enslave our spiritual walk. If you find that struggle of unforgiveness, blame, jealousy or condemnation of others within you, work to extend forgiveness and continue to release the offense to God. It's often a process, but don't allow wrongdoing to drive your responses. It can only lead to difficulty. When we take up our cross and choose to forgive, the promises of God's Word will enlighten our natures with the character of Christ. True forgiveness unlocks spiritual authority as Paul promises, *For the message of the cross is foolishness to those who are perishing, but to us who are being saved it is the power of God* (1 Corinthians 1:18).

THE RELEASE:

Jesus was the ultimate victor! He made Himself of no reputation by submitting to brutal beating, desertion, denial by His closest friends, and humiliation of crucifixion as a criminal. At the height of the pain and agony, He cried out, *"Father, forgive them, for they do not know what they do"* (Luke 23:34). The cry was an audible ticket to the forever courtrooms of heaven. Despite the physical and emotional pain, no root of bitterness would ever block His forever love to and for us all. Forgiveness is the key to freedom. John says, *By this we know love, because He laid down His life for us* (1 John 3:16).

The forever access to God's love was secured by Jesus not taking on offense, but rather freely offering forgiveness and laying down His life for us. We, too, as imitators of Jesus, must forgive, especially as end-time narratives unfold. Jesus warns us of lawless times, *And then many will be offended, will betray one another, and will hate one another* (Matthew 24:10).

When challenged and the agony of conflict and rejection hits, what can we do? I have learned over the years it is best to handle conflict when it arises, or I sense the antagonism in the atmosphere. It is like an alligator in a swamp; it will disappear, but sooner or later, it will raise its ugly head to bite you, and it will hurt. I have also learned that speaking or reacting out of frustration rarely produces any fruit and can get you in trouble. We need to be centered in Him when we respond to conflict. It may relieve the pressure cooker to react, but frequently it does not lead to healthy intervention. Holding in the frustration or anger does not help either. *Life and death are in the power of the tongue* (Proverbs 18:21); and this fact is Truth!

I had to confront some issues with a leader in the ministry who wielded a lot of manipulation and challenged authority. The disruptive problems took me eight months deal with. Is that a response to conflict? Yes. It may take time to resolve conflict and it can certainly take time to get our emotions under control. During that time, I had time to commit my emotions to the Lord and seek His face. Eventually, the situation came to an obvious head. I was thankful for the advice I received during the preceding months to approach it with a "sound mind." The process of seeking the Lord and waiting for a more measured way to respond opened a pathway for forgiveness in my heart. The relief I felt going through the actual process of confrontation then carried a more substantial weight of resolution than if I had just responded in frustration at some point along the way. Today, the relationship and healthy collaboration is fully restored. When offense and unforgiveness threaten to lock us down, try the following check list:

- When we have been left out or rejected we continue to persevere and think positively towards others, Galatians 2:20, Philippians 4:8-9.
- When betrayed, we forgive, Matthew 6:14-15; Mark 11:25.
- When our authority has been usurped or challenged or negated, we have sought Your face and kept our integrity, Psalm 25:21.
- When reputation has been defiled, we have not sought recompense but trusted in You, Psalm 37:1-6, 34-40.
- When oppressed, we endured and waited for Your deliverance and timing, Psalm 9:7-10; 103:5-6.
- When misrepresented and misjudged, we kept silent and waited for your justice, Psalm 34:17-22; 1 Peter 5:10.
- When we sinned, we confessed, Romans 2:4.
- When we presumed, You challenged us to set us back on the right course and we obeyed, Psalms 19:13.
- When those who persecuted us repented, we sought ways to restore them, Galatians 6:1.
- When even in the shadow of death, we have feared and trusted You, Psalm 23; Psalm 40:4.

As we release forgiveness and grace towards ourselves and others, it becomes a sacrifice of self that harnesses the character of Christ in us. Our feet miss the traps that could entangle our journey. God looks down and says, "There is a vessel I can trust." Watch the spiritual doors open, your prayers be answered, and the God-ordained opportunities present themselves. Forgiveness leads to spiritual maturity and authority. No longer are we slaves, but Jesus' friends whom He can trust.

THE REWARD:

Adoption brings us boldly before the throne of grace, *Let us therefore come boldly to the throne of grace, that we may obtain mercy and find grace to help in time of need* (Hebrews 4:16). The throne of grace is known by the adopted sons and daughters. It has nothing to do with our performance but everything to do with our hearts. It makes no excuses for sin but makes provision to remove the stumbling blocks and stones for those willing to see clearly, and who want their paths to be made straight. In such a spirit, we can serve the Lord with joy, without fear of reproach or obligation. How does the Spirit of adoption work through us? Paul describes it in Romans 8:12-17:

> *Therefore, brethren, we are debtors—not to the flesh, to live according to the flesh. For if you live according to the flesh you will die; but if by the Spirit you put to death the deeds of the body, you will live. For as many as are led by the Spirit of God, these are sons of God.* **For you did not receive the spirit of bondage again to fear, but you received the Spirit of adoption by whom we cry out, "Abba, Father."** *The Spirit Himself bears witness with our spirit that we are children of God, and if children, then heirs—heirs of God and joint heirs with Christ, if indeed we suffer with Him, that we may also be glorified together.*

Through these verses, Paul affirms how the Spirit of adoption removes the bondage of fear. When operating in adoption, fear of man and its grip will give way to the fear of the Lord. Wisdom and inner peace in the face of conflict will be the result.

- *Fear of Lord is the beginning of wisdom* (Job 28:28; Psalm 111:10; Proverbs 1:7, 9:10, 15:33).

- *The Spirit of the Lord shall rest upon Him, the Spirit of wisdom and understanding, the Spirit of counsel and might, the Spirit of knowledge and of the fear of the Lord* (Isaiah 11:2).

When the Spirit of adoption is at work in us, it assures our spirits of the Father's love and faithfulness towards us. Russell Moore explains the "Abba" cry in his exposition on Romans 8:12-17:

> "The text says that the Holy Spirit Himself bears witness together or alongside our renewed spirit, both testify that we are the children of God! In Hebrew culture, the testimony of two witnesses was required to establish a truth, and here we have two witnesses: that of our innermost being which is crying out "ABBA, FATHER", and that of the Holy Spirit. What a double testimony![2]"

Paul relays to the Ephesian Church that through this Spirit of adoption we will reap significant benefits:

> *The Father of glory, may give to you the spirit of wisdom and revelation in the knowledge of Him, the eyes of your understanding being enlightened, that you may know what is the hope of His calling, what are the riches of the glory of His inheritance in the saints, and what is the exceeding greatness of His power toward us who believe, according to the working of His mighty power which He worked in Christ when He raised Him from the dead and seated Him at His right hand in the heavenly places, far above all principality and power and might and dominion, and every name that is named, not only in this age but also in that which is to come* (Ephesians 1:17-20).

When the Spirit of adoption is at work in us, from this passage we access the following:

- ♦ Wisdom, v.17
- ♦ Revelation, v 17
- ♦ Knowledge of Him, v. 17

- ◆ Eyes of understanding would be enlightened v. 18
- ◆ Hope v. 18
- ◆ His power v. 19

These verses clearly point to the fact that we will not see clearly without the Spirit of adoption working in our lives. Our view of God will be stunted. A.W. Tozer, noted pastor and author, said,

> "The low view of God entertained almost universally among Christians is the cause of a hundred lesser evils everywhere among us... The decline of the knowledge of the holy has brought on our troubles. A rediscovery of the majesty of God will go a long way toward curing them."[3]

We must work to remove the stumbling blocks, clear our heads to see the hand of the Lord and ponder the Truth to make our heart a home for God to reside. For out of the abundance of the heart our mouths will speak (Luke 6:45).

RUNNING WITH ENDURANCE:

In these days of adversity, every work of God will have its trials and challenges—all the more important for us to build our personal and corporate prayer lives. The challenges, *pushbacks,* and tests God allows are not without purpose. Paul promises, *No temptation has overtaken you except such as is common to man; but God is faithful, who will not allow you to be tempted beyond what you are able, but with the temptation will also make the way of escape, that you may be able to bear it* (1 Corinthians 10:13).

Roger Heuser relays this battle, "The examples of testing in Scripture illustrates that the most severe tests come to those who are the most faithful. One thing is sure; however, the testing is not meant as punishment for ineffectiveness. Rather the testing is intended as graduation to greater faithfulness and effectiveness. It is meant as a seal of God's approval upon the work that is already done."[4]

In fact, the higher the call, the greater the challenges will be. Why? God allows them to test our character. When tests come, discouragement, anger, hurt, frustration can take over our spirit and soul. God, on the other hand, allows and desires them to draw us closer to Him. Per Paul's exhortation to the Corinthians, everyone gets tested, 1 Corinthians 10:13. Ronald Heifetz states the principle well, "Your management of an attack, more than the substance of the accusation, determines your fate."[5] When you are tested, know there is a God who cares for you. Circumstances are a concern, but the development of our character will carry the "eternal weight of glory" (2 Corinthians 4:17). When times get tough, don't give up! More than likely, His promises are right around the corner for those who persevere.

In addition to developing our character, God uses attacks and tests to increase our resolve, and develop wisdom in stewarding our call. Paul exhorts in Romans 12:2: *And do not be conformed to this world, but be transformed by the renewing of your mind.* Thompson further explains that the brain can "create new neurons, make new neural connections and prune those it no longer needs,"[6] making it malleable and adaptable. He states, "To have the mind of Christ, therefore, requires that we encounter an integrating Spirit who searches us and allows us to know him as we are searched---as we are known."[7] In other words, there are actual physical changes that take place in our brain during these seasons of testing that give us stronger capabilities and resiliency for future tests.

Medical research corroborates that an area in your brain known as the hippocampus creates new neurons influencing certain types of learning and memory.[8] It is a process, but the change can be real. We simply have to train our mind to think on good things as Paul exhorts:

> *Finally, brethren, whatever things are true, whatever things are noble, whatever things are just, whatever things are pure, whatever things are lovely, whatever things are of good report, if there is any virtue and if there is anything praiseworthy—meditate on these things. The things which you*

learned and received and heard and saw in me, these do, and the God of peace will be with you (Philippians 4:8-9).

Our *headsets* can change!

Tests expand our capacity to endure more substantial challenges in the future. Quinn explains, "The hero's journey is a story of individual transformation, a change of identity. In embarking on the journey, we must leave the world of certainty. We must courageously journey to a strange place where there are many risks, and much is at stake, a place where there are new problems that require us to think in new ways."[9]

Heuser states, "Not only must faithful ministry be tested, but it is also often resisted. Without resistance, there can be no acceptance of the ostentatious and unbelievable promises that God makes to the called one."[10] James 1:2 exhorts, *Count it all joy when you fall into various trials knowing that the testing of your faith produces patience. But let patience have its perfect work, that you may be perfect and complete, lacking nothing.* In these times of testing, God makes it clear in His Word that he seeks to strengthen our hearts and align us with our identity (see also Psalm 27:14, 31:24, 41:3, Isaiah 35:3, 41:10, Zechariah 10:12; Luke 22:32, Hebrews 12:12, 1 Peter 5:10).

Once we recognize and identify with our call, the resources of heaven are released as Ephesians 1:3 declares, *Blessed be the God and Father of our Lord Jesus Christ who has blessed us with every spiritual blessing in the heavenly places.* When we respond to the tests in life and take the heat, our spiritual muscle is exercised and developed, preparing us to respond to future tests with resolve and Godly character. In other words, it is not wise to take someone off the playground and make them president of the United States or someone out of high school and make them CEO of a major corporation. There is a process of testing God allows in honing our gifts and abilities into a character that can steward His call forward.

Leaders who submit to the testing of God pave the way for others to follow. Being secure in their gifts and calling, such leaders foster environments that empower others. Moses was eighty years old when he was summoned to speak to Pharaoh, Exodus 7:7. His life was tested and tried from his birth onwards. As he responded to the challenges, God handed him stewardship of a national deliverance for Israel. Not only that, for forty years he also led a million-and-a-half people in the desert, eating manna, to their final destination in the Promised Land. Such a call required character training in the most profound ways. In his book on leadership, Sherwood Lingenfelter expresses the process well: "Leading then, is inspiring people who participate with you in a community of trust to follow you."[11]

Centering on Christ is a foundation for a productive life that bears much fruit. Jesus promises, *"I am the vine, you are the branches. He who abides in Me, and I in him, bears much fruit; for without Me you can do nothing"* (John 15:5). The inward development of a leader eventually feeds into the outward expression and fulfillment of the call of God. The apostle John exhorts, *Love has been perfected among us in this: that we may have boldness in the day of judgment; because as He is, so are we in this world. There is no fear in love, but perfect love casts out fear* (1John 4:17-18). The ultimate expression of our identity in Christ is made real through God's love when expressed and received by others in a wounded and broken world.

SUMMARY:

We are in days when adversity, challenge and headwinds of moral decline are begging the Church to bend our knees and bow our heads to cry out for God's mercy and intervention. Withstanding the threshing floor of character development and being sent to encourage the body of Christ, visionaries carrying the "House of Prayer" mandate are rising. The task requires both personal character development and sensitivity to the Body of Christ's corporate condition. Those answering the call are highly tested. The Global Watch has developed a set of "Core Values" based on biblical concepts that promote a healthy corporate atmosphere. These core values have kept relationships healthy and the community alive. They are concepts to live by in any church or community venturing into the corporate prayer expression.

Though the hearts of men may find it challenging to make the adaptive change to prioritize prayer, we are finding those who carry the vision relentless. Their calling is now more readily heard in a Church being increasingly challenged by the headwinds of turmoil, and moral decline. Through a remnant, those called are persistent in their relationship with Jesus and moving towards intentional and effective relationship with one another. As Hebrews 10:23-25 envisions, *Let us hold fast the confession of our hope without wavering, for He who promised is faithful. And let us consider one another in order to stir up love and good works, not forsaking the assembling of ourselves together, as is the manner of some, but exhorting one another, and so much the more as you see the Day approaching.* The Day is approaching, and He is preparing His alert and ready Bride.

DISCUSSION QUESTIONS:

1. With increasing social and cultural adversity opposing the Church, it is imperative that we walk in the fulness of our position of "Adoption." Using the list on page 122, take a moment for self-evaluation. Are any of these points threatening your authority and position in the Lord?

2. We all face tests and challenges that can put us on the threshing floor of God's character development. What are steps we can take to help us be victorious in such times? (Compare Romans 8:38-39 with Philippians 4:8-9)

PRAYER POINTS:

1. Declare scriptures over your personal challenges. These challenges may include complacency and need for a renewed heart, discouragement, fear, self-condemnation, critical spirit, sin entrapments, roots of bitterness towards yourself or others, all of which separate us from God.

2. Renew your mind with scriptures that directly address your challenge

ACTION STEPS:

Commit to memory scriptures that encourage your spiritual growth. Doing so speaks life into "dry bones" and will strengthen your spiritual journey.

9

THE REFORM: PREPARE THE WAY

Behold, I will send you Elijah the prophet
before the coming of the great and dreadful day of the Lord.
And he will turn the hearts of the fathers to the children,
and the hearts of the children to their fathers.
Malachi 4:5-6

This chapter relays various expressions and insights where corporate prayer is igniting churches and communities with revelation and transformational power.

CORPORATE PRAYER/EKKLESIA AS A PLACE OF IDENTITY FOR THE CHURCH:
Pastor Greg Simas, Founder Convergence House of Prayer, Fremont, CA
https://convergencehop.org

Hendrick Kraemer, a Bishop in Denmark during World War II, described the panic that overtook the clergy of his diocese as the Nazis marched in to take possession of their country. As priests and pastors gathered to his home, they asked, "What shall we do?" He answered, "First, we must ask who we are! If we know who we are, then we will know what to do."

Jesus said, *"I will build my Church, and the gates of Hades will not overcome it"* Matthew 16:18). It was at the Gates of Hades that Jesus releases two of the most significant revelations in the New Testament. First, the declaration that **He is the Christ.** And second, that **He will build His Church**. The word here for the church is Ekklesia and should be translated as "assembly." The agency Jesus chooses to move through the Gates of Hades with is the Ekklesia - the legislative ruling assembly in His day.

The agency with whom Jesus chooses to move through the Gates of Hades is the Ekklesia. The Passion Translation makes the meaning of the "church," or rather the "Ekklesia" clear: *"And this truth of who I am will be the bedrock foundation on which I will build My church—My legislative assembly..."* (Emphasis added) – (Matthew 16:18).

Jesus is calling forth His legislative assembly. We must know what this means and join Him. If we fail to discern what He is building, I'm afraid we come up short and end up creating something that He is not.

Jesus brought a Kingdom, His Kingdom. Isaiah prophesied that the government will be on His shoulders (Is. 9:6). His Kingdom is then governmental, not religious. It's active, not passive. We are called to join Him in legislating His Kingdom on earth as it is in heaven (Mt. 6:10).

As a legislative assembly, the ekklesia can be defined as the local expression of heaven transforming every sphere of society on earth, bringing God's world into this one. The Church then is a gathering of people, living stones, of the ekklesia. They are the called-out ones who govern from a place of intercession to shift the atmospheres of cities with the end goal of winning people to Jesus, and destroying the works of the devil.

Living and doing ministry in the San Francisco Bay Area has its challenges. It's hectic, liberal, the cost of living is substantial, and the endless opportunities for entertainment compete with Kingdom priorities.

We've felt the disappointment of calling corporate prayer gatherings or extended fasts only to have a limited amount of people engage. We wrestled with trying to come up with a solution for the lack of participation. Why aren't our people showing up? How do we get our people to pray corporately? What can we do better?

We eventually discovered the lack of people showing up to our corporate prayer meetings was more due to an absence of identity rather than spiritual lethargy. Our prayer meetings have grown as we teach our people about who they are as Christ's ekklesia; followers of Jesus called out and summoned to legislate heaven to earth. When our members discover who they are as Christ's ekklesia, they know what they must do, legislate through prayer. Our prayer meetings have grown out of a place of identity, not necessarily necessity. Prayer is now central, intentional, and powerful.

As Christ's ekklesia, we partner from a position of sonship and legislate from a posture of intercession. We joyfully co-labor with Jesus, the Great Intercessor, to see His Kingdom come and His will to be done on earth as it is in heaven.

A LOCAL CHURCH EXPRESSION:

Sheldon Kidwell: Bay City Church - Cape Town South Africa
http://www.baycc.co.za/

I had the privilege of being handed leadership of our church community from my father, who had planted and pastored the church for 20 years, and in which I served all during that time. I was a worshipper at heart and had a genuine desire to see the spirit of the Tabernacle of David made real within a church community in the form of ongoing corporate prayer and worship. I always believed that prayer and worship were closely linked and didn't play separate roles, whether for the individual believer or in the corporate church setting.

If we were to become a model as a community, we'd need to have something to show for it so others could see and learn. With a desire in my heart to see an entire community take up this challenge for prayer and worship to arise, the journey of learning to express and articulate all that was in my heart had begun. I quickly learned that the foundation for corporate prayer is to create a culture and lifestyle rather than a program to follow. Establishing such an atmosphere is best birthed from a place of revelation and conviction, and that we, the Ekklesia, are called to first honor the majesty of our King before any program is established.

The global pandemic of 2020 was a demanding year for many in every facet of life and society. However, it was also the Church's greatest opportunity to be flexible; and help people through difficult and unpredictable times. This season re-awakened desires of years past to again see a people arise in prayer. The challenges of COVID 19 positioned us as an eldership and leadership team. We were ready to receive and embrace the call for prayer to be built upon the deep heart connections. I'd also learned that if the leadership doesn't model this for the community, it will become another program to maintain.

When I presented the vision of establishing ongoing prayer watches through communities of prayer to the leadership team, there was a resounding "yes" within the room. Apart from helping iron out a few logistical questions, people were ready to run with the vision. Starting with the leaders, we were able to establish twelve watches. These were corporate prayer/worship gatherings at different times each week. We divided into clusters of twos and threes—these groups connected via online programs like Zoom, WhatsApp, or in person.

Establishing a set time, or "rhythm," of prayer for a community does force people to adjust to ensure prayer becomes a priority. But, most important is the commitment to each other ensuring we sustain this and don't allow the flesh to make decisions for us. After a few weeks, in reports back from leaders, many said they were tired, and the thought of gathering for prayer was challenging. But once they had committed and prayed together, they were encouraged and refreshed. There is a lesson in that! The Spirit is willing but the flesh is weak.

As pastors and leaders, we are all aware of the prayer meeting that is the least attended in the church. Communities in prayer, on the other hand, makes Acts 2:42 come alive. When people experience such a community, commitment naturally follows.

When the purpose of gathering in prayer is to encounter Him, Heaven partners with us. By the Spirit, the manifest presence of God brings life, healing, faith, and boldness to every heart. Prayer and worship establish us as individuals with the altar of our hearts honoring Him, but corporately, we, as the ekklesia, establish an altar of His presence in the supernatural realm over communities, cities, and regions. From this place, as priests in the tabernacle, we position ourselves to legislate order in the heavens so that what we bind on earth will be bound in heaven and what we loose on earth will be loosed in heaven (Mattew16 & 18). What gets set in order in the Spirit will manifest in the natural.

Keys to establish corporate prayer:
Have a clear vision and mandate from the Lord

It may sound strange to require vision or a mandate when we speak of prayer. You would think we all have this, but church leadership needs to answer this: What motivates or mobilizes you and your people to pray? If vision is driven by any form of works, striving, wants, comparison or competitiveness, the motivation is selfish, and it will never sustain a prayer community. If, however, the motivation comes from a place of conviction and carries the heart of Jesus, it will be a sustaining and motivating factor. Conviction comes from revelation of Jesus. He is the head of the Church.

Your personal abilities, or gifts, come from Him. They are given to ensure the people you lead will be properly discipled by you, and will mature for their own works of service.

Having a Jesus-centered vision for any community and living with this conviction, we are in the right place to see corporate prayer, and consequently the Church, flourish and succeed. Paul proclaims Christ crucified in his message to the Corinthians so that our "faith might not rest on the wisdom of men but in the power of God" (1 Corinthians 2:5). We fully rest and rely on the Spirit to lead us.

Spirit led, not program driven

Jesus mandated His disciples to wait. He directed them, "Wait for the Promise of the Father—you shall receive power when the Holy Spirit has come upon you" (Acts 1:4,8). Such empowering is the work of the Holy Spirit alive within us, enabling us to achieve things beyond our own natural abilities. Motivating people to pray requires us to walk by the Spirit. In many cases, we see the apostles laying hands on the believers to receive the Holy Spirit through the book of Acts. Without His infilling, we very easily follow religious traditions of duty; but living and leading *by the Spirit* yields a delight that sustains and gives us life. Through the complete work of Jesus, our walk with Him does not operate from earth to heaven; rather, it is from heaven to earth. We walk in the power of the Holy Spirit knowing we are seated with Christ in heavenly places as His co-laborers. As Jesus prayed, *That they all may be one, as You Father, are in Me, and I in You* (John 17:21).

One in heart and mind

At the beginning of Acts 2:1 we read how the disciples "were all with one accord in one place" (KJV). They were of the same heart and mind. Unity has been a buzzword over the last decade, as the church works hard at being unified. Being one in the Lord marks our starting point. It is possible because of the finished work of Jesus. We are unified and need to ensure that we walk and live it out by being a community of the Spirit first as Paul exhorts: *Therefore, from now on, we regard no one according to the flesh. Even though we have known Christ according to the flesh, yet now we know Him thus no longer* (2 Corinthians 5:16). From this place, there is joint accountability to ensure community in prayer is sustained.

Some Practical Steps: These are just some practical points to help facilitate the implementation of corporate prayer in your community.
1. Keep a set time, whether it is daily, weekly, or monthly depending on the individual and corporate prayer strength.
2. Start with leadership. They can model the way forward.
3. Start small with shorter times of prayer if necessary; it will grow. As relationships develop, hearts connect and

prayer deepens. By establishing set times for prayer, a rhythm will develop feeding into a climate, or culture, of prayer.

4. Ensure the foundation of the gathering is for the purpose of prayer and worship.

5. Explore different sizes and shapes of groups: All generation "ekklesia" gatherings along with men's, women's, youth groups. Groups can be centered around specific topics such as praying for technology, business, government, etc.

6. Develop a communication system to get feedback and share ideas.

7. Don't let groups become exclusive or closed.

The benefits and effects of corporate prayer in your community:

1. It places the Church in a position to receive God's transformational power and work through the congregation to impact the community/city at large!

2. Establishing a corporate prayer time is an expression of love for—and commitment to—the Lord, thus drawing His attention, *Draw near to God and He will draw near to you* (James 4:8). The Church will come under the blessing of God.

3. Relationships build as people share ideas and are motivated to pray and a healthy sense of community is set into motion.

4. When someone joins your local church, corporate prayer sessions offer a place to develop within the larger community, with a unique place for them to mature and grow.

5. Building corporate prayer that spans communities establishes you as an ekklesia and gives you governmental authority.

a. You are now not reactive to the schemes and works of the enemy, but proactive on the wall. Paul, in Ephesians 6, speaks of standing—that's standing in the right place with the right armor, and not being caught off guard. No need to frantically gather a prayer meeting for an emergency; people are already positioned.

b. Prayer points can be sent to the prayer watches when the community, city or nation needs focused prayer.

6. You truly start seeing Acts 2:42 come alive through prayer, fellowship, sound teaching and the breaking of bread.

Our encouragement to local churches is to position yourselves from the place of encountering Jesus. From the place of His presence, the Ekklesia will return to its true biblical foundation as a *house of prayer*.

THE LOCAL CONGREGATION AS A HOUSE OF PRAYER
Karen Davis: Co-Founder/Worship Director, Kehilat HaCarmel, Israel
www.carmelcongregation.org.il

When the Lord positioned our congregational worship center on the highest point of Mount Carmel, we understood the vital role that worship and prayer were to have in building our Israeli congregation and in advancing the kingdom of God in northern Israel. When our worship center was dedicated in 1998, a plaque engraved with Isaiah 56:7, "My house shall be called a house of prayer for all nations," was placed in our foyer as a continuing reminder of our calling as a congregation to be a house of prayer.

Also, built into the very bedrock under the main sanctuary is our "Elijah Prayer Cave," dedicated solely to worship and prayer. The combined ministry of worship and prayer ("intercessory worship") is an integral function of the congregation. It is essential to the outworking of evangelism, discipleship, and our humanitarian outreaches to confront the spiritual powers of darkness that hinder our people from salvation in Messiah Yeshua and threaten the very survival of our nation.

Several years ago, we instituted the "Mt Carmel Worship Watch" with intercessory and devotional watches taking place in the main sanctuary, as well as the Elijah Prayer Cave. These watches are mainly led by the worship and prayers leaders of the congregation, but intercessors from the nations who desire to stand with the local body in the Land are welcomed.

Corporate prayer and worship are woven into the daily and weekly rhythm of our community life, both in our physical, as well as Zoom gatherings. As we continue to "make known to the principalities and powers the manifold wisdom of God" (Eph. 3:10), through our corporate prophetic declarations and intercessions, the heavens are indeed beginning to open over Mount Carmel.

A NATIONAL HOUSE OF PRAYER:
Jenny Hagger, Director AHOPFAN Inc., Australian House of Prayer for All Nations
www.ahopfan.com

My city of Adelaide in South Australia was founded in 1836. It is known as the City of Churches because it was the first free settlement colony in Australia, allowing religious freedom amongst its pioneers.

In the last thirty years, the Lord has moved powerfully to raise a movement of prayer, but it has found expression outside the walls of the established church. It began when I had an unexpected encounter with the Lord in 1987, in which He instructed me to build a prayer center for intercessors in preparation for the Holy Spirit's latter-day rain (James 5:7-8). The Lord revealed that revival would come to Australia, and with it a great outpouring to the nations, and He gave me the biblical pattern of Noah building the ark according to God's command and specifications, even though Noah had never seen rain. The words of Hebrews 11:6 burned within me: *But without faith it is impossible to please Him, for he who comes to God must believe that He is; and that He is the rewarder of those who diligently seek Him.*

The mandate was Isaiah 56:7 – *"For my house shall be called a house of prayer for all nations."* We had no known template to follow, nor did we know anyone else establishing a house of prayer. Further, the pastors in our city were reluctant to give us any support, struggling at first to understand the concept of people from different denominations coming together to pray.

The vision was officially established in 1990. We began to develop a library emphasizing historical, geographical, political and religious aspects of nations. Today LASREC (our Library and Strategic Research Center) is a major key in developing our watchmen and intercessors.

Since those early days, the Lord has led us to open three houses of prayer: our main center in the Adelaide Hills, the Lighthouse Prayer Tower in the center of our city, and Kingsgate Haven, a house of prayer with accommodation on Kangaroo Island off the coast of South Australia. Two years ago, we established the South Pacific House of Prayer.

We have mobilized teams to join us on local, national, and overseas assignments. Others have gathered to pray at strategic sites around our city regularly, prayer-walk our streets, and meet weekly at Parliament House to pray. Corporate prayer is a key part of our Father's House fellowship on Sundays.

For the past 20 years, we have held Revival SA, monthly city-wide worship and prayer meetings in the heart of the city, testifying to Matthew 18:20: *For where two or three are gathered in my name, I am there in the midst of them.*

Throughout the years, from across all denominations and ethnicities, up to 300 people regularly attended these meetings, experiencing powerful corporate prayer as led by the Holy Spirit. Jesus is in the midst and no two sessions have ever been the same. The outpouring of love for Jesus and each other is palpable and overrides all the religious and cultural traditions that could separate us. In places of corporate prayer, God does what the world can never do! He binds us together in oneness because our eyes are focused on Him, the King of Glory.

Romans 8:34 tells us that Jesus sits at the right hand of God interceding for us. There is great depth in these words. Prayer starts in the throne room! It is not a dry religious activity that we should fulfill but a glorious entry into the intercession of Christ as led by the Holy Spirit. Jesus, when on earth, taught His disciples to pray "Our Father" indicating a corporateness as we gather to pray in the Spirit of the Tabernacle of David.

All nations are invited to join Him in His house of prayer, to pray for all nations, *Isaiah 56:7*. What a stunning mandate He has given us!

A GLOBAL CALL: THE GLOBAL WATCH:
Susan and Frederic Rowe, Founders, The Global Watch
www.theglobalwatch.com

Understanding the foundations of any ministry are essential in knowing how to engage and sustain it for longevity and growth. The following is a summary of the visionary, prophetic foundations for the "Global Watch." Amos 3:7 states, *Surely the Lord God does nothing unless He reveals His secret to His servants the prophets.* The Global Watch birthed out of a genuine call of God for the hour in which we live. It is a call to build communities of prayer from local expressions to global connections.

Though physicians by trade, God had convicted both of us of our prayerlessness after reading "Could you not Tarry One Hour" by Larry Lee.[1] What happened through this conviction, began a life-changing

_____

146

journey. We stepped forward in our church and began to build up our personal prayer lives and corporate prayer expression.

In 1998, we were contacted by national prayer leadership to convene a "Call to Prayer" for California due to rising concerns towards our state. Chuck Pierce released a catalytic prophetic word calling for the "Watch" during the gathering. The word released a powerful outpouring of the Holy Spirit amongst the attendees. Amid the spiritual impartation, the call to *watch* was indelibly imprinted on our hearts. As a result, the *Watch of the Lord* became a quest and journey in our hearts and lives. We have held a form of the "Watch" in our region in California ever since. It has taken on various forms, each with its lessons and rewards. All expressions have journeyed towards the revelation of what the "Watch" is and the role of watchmen today.

In October of 2000, in a time of intense prayer over the particularly vicious warfare I was under, I had an open vision. In the vision, I was set on the streets of New York and saw two giant towers explode into rubble. The debris was comprised of steel frames like a building that had collapsed. Suddenly, a giant pair of hands came out of the sky. They scooped up the rubble, shaping and forming it in its hands. The hands opened. In them was a large clock tower. The clock tower was the image of *Big Ben.*

The vision was particularly alarming for two reasons. First, it was very clear. Second, there was a distinct paradigm shift in the atmosphere as the warfare broke and replaced by the peace of God. Over the ensuing weeks, while seeking the Lord about the meaning of the vision, I was drawn to 2 Kings 11. As Big Ben is an icon of global time, the scripture caught my attention. It relays a story of how a national "Watch" under the leadership of Jehoiada the priest, saved Joash, a true heir to David's throne, from being killed by Athaliah who destroyed "all the royal heirs" (2 Kings 11:1). Their coordinated efforts saved the line of David and secured the future for the appearance of Jesus and fulfillment of the Davidic covenant, 2 Samuel 7:8-16.

Pondering the vision and scripture, the thought of a "Global Watch" began to emerge. Then, 09/11/2001 happened. The rubble from the collapsed towers was a mirror image of what I had seen in the open vision. God was certainly sending a message! An end-time birth pang had just burst onto the global scene; the Lord began to confirm the concept of a "Global Watch."

During the ensuing years, I pondered the concept of a "Global Watch," mostly in my heart. As the attacks of 9/11 impacted world history, I knew the open vision was not just about September 11; it was about something in the future carrying global weight. My heart was riveted towards the 2 Kings 11 message and how the "Watch of the Lord" prepared Israel to receive the true king Joash. Similarly today, as God did for Israel in 2 Kings 11, He is now preparing the earth for the "return of the King."

Propelled by the vision, we worked on building the "Watch" constructs, holding weekly worship gatherings in our local community first. Occasionally I talked to others about the concept of a Global Watch. There was immediate interest, but neither my husband, Fred, nor I felt that the relationships or time were right until I went to a small gathering of ministry leaders with global interest at the All-Nations Conference Center (ANCC) in London England, in August 2015. At that meeting, the Lord said, "Speak it out." So, I did. Others immediately took interest and caught the vision, and the group began to work on the construct.

Interestingly, at the ANCC meeting, word came that Big Ben had ticked ahead seven seconds. And IXXI (9/11 in Roman numerals) appeared in the sky—a sign and wonder? That is how it has been. God has confirmed, through unusual signs, His affirmations aimed towards building the ramparts of the Watch, the communities of contending prayer, at every significant decision point. (You can read more at the following link: https://www.theglobalwatch.com/prophetic-history.html).

In April, 2016, the call to the Watch led us on a preliminary journey to the historical place for watchmen, Herrnhut, Germany. The name *Herrnhut* means the "Lord's Watch." The purpose of the journey was to scout out the possibility of holding a prayer summit on the 290th year anniversary, August 13, 2017, of an historic outpouring of the Holy Spirit leading to over 100 years of 24/7 prayer.

Traveling the back roads of former East Germany, we finally landed in the quiet streets of Herrnhut in the late afternoon, April 27, 2016. As we stepped out of the car, we were greeted by our host. Looking down the street, however, a rather diplomatic-looking group of people were walking in our direction. Our host greeted us and remarked, "That is the president of Germany, Joachin Gauch!" Our curiosity was most assuredly peaked. We followed the core of distinguished people up to "God's Acre," the graveyard for the Moravian church and history-making leaders and missionaries. Staying a respectful distance away, we simply waited, pondering this extraordinary chance meeting. Then one of the entourage approached and invited us to meet the president. Of course, we gratefully accepted! This encounter led to meeting the president of Germany, who welcomed us into the nation, right at the tombstone of Count Nicholas von Zinzendorf!

The Global Watch reflects the revival seed of Herrnhut. With the history of the community that Herrnhut flourished in, our vision is to establish communities of committed prayer that will empower the Church for a three-fold mission:

1. Contend for the destiny of nations and Israel (Isaiah 46:9-10; Psalm 33:10-12; Matthew 25:32-33).
2. Release the final frontiers of the global harvest (John 4:35; Romans 11:25-26, Matthew 28:19).
3. Ignite revival for the end-time glory of the Church (Amos 9:11-12; Isaiah 62:6-7; Isaiah 56:6-7; Isaiah 52:8).

We are thankful the Lord has taken His time to teach us the art of warfare from the vantage point of both the ramparts and the trenches. The construct of the Global Watch is entirely different today than it would have been in 2001. Though this summary just scratches the surface, we pray it inspires your hearts to respond to the call of God.

Run with the vision. It shall tarry no more (Habakkuk 2:1-3). It was Jesus who exhorted His disciples to *Take heed, watch and pray; for you do not know when the time is* (Mark 13:33). You can join the Global Watch online by visiting the website noted above.

What does it mean to *watch?* Strengthen the relationships around you, commit to pray, build community, communicate and share with one another, connect across the nations, and watch God move. The time is now. The Body is becoming the Bride, awakened, ready and alert! The true King is coming. No person is too small or ministry too big to take part. Participation does not interfere with any person's call, ministry, or church leadership structure but functions to guard and protect one another. The Watch will prepare the way for His rule and reign!

DISCUSSION QUESTIONS:

1. Assembly," "Legislative," and "Governmental," are all used in describing the Ekklesia—the Church. Discuss what this understanding of God's church is in comparison to your current local context. Use Matthew 16:18 and Matthew 6:10 as your guide.
2. Discuss what role Peter played in recognizing who Jesus was in the subsequent release of the identity of the Church? What role does the ministry of recognition play today in the Church?
3. Discuss how we can actively engage in empowering the church through the ministry of recognition?
4. Discuss key components of an Ekklesia? What role does corporate prayer play in such a community?

PRAYER POINTS:

1. Pray for effectual doors of ministry to open for your gifts and abilities to be used to advance the Kingdom. 1 Corinthians 16:9
2. Pray for strategies of corporate prayer to be received and implemented in local church bodies.

ACTION STEPS:

1. Take steps to encourage someone who deserves recognition and bless them.

2. Jesus also commanded us to "Bless those who curse you." Take steps to reach out to those who have hindered or hurt you to acknowledge their role in the kingdom and bless them.

10

THE RETURN: WATCH AND PRAY

Your watchmen shall lift up their voices,
With their voices they shall sing together;
For they shall see eye to eye
When the LORD brings back Zion.
Isaiah 52:8

Throughout history, there are certain "set" times when God highlights specific themes previously held in relative obscurity and releases a fresh revelation of their full intent. Today, as we face pandemics, natural disasters of greater intensity and frequency, and wars and rumors of war escalate, the term to "watch" and the role of the "Watchman" is such a theme. Jesus' exhortation to His disciples when He found them sleeping in the Garden was to "watch and pray" (Matthew 26:41). In other words, the call to watch is distinct from prayer alone. The Greek word for *watch* is *grēgoreuō*. It means "to take heed lest through remission and indolence some destructive calamity suddenly overtake one."[1] To actively watch lends a vigilance to our prayers. It connotes alertness to not only our personal prayer concerns but a diligent searching of the spiritual horizon to engage and declare the purposes of God. As the end-time narrative unfolds, God is re-digging the ancient role of the watchman with a heralding call to His Church.

Watchmen are spoken of throughout the Bible from Genesis to Revelation. They have a key role in the Kingdom and the Church. Everyone is called to pray. But watchmen have a special role in prayer and in the Kingdom, particularly in the end-times. We are in the midst of huge governmental shifts in the nations. **We are in a war!** Provoked by the discomfort, the prayer movement is shifting into a watchmen movement. Out of individual prayer rooms, war rooms, and stance as intercessors, the relentless watchmen of Isaiah 62:6 are emerging. God is calling forth watchmen worldwide who will stand with Him in the days of increasing adversity. They will contend for His Kingdom and covenant purposes "on earth as it is in Heaven" (Matthew 6:10).

Additionally, studying the end-times and the biblical narrative lends a unique revelation of Jesus' nature that inspires faith and hope, particularly in troubled times. As trials will surely increase, worshiping and seeking Jesus' redeeming, loving character amid judgments can ignite weary hearts. Isaiah promises, *For when Your judgments are in the earth, the inhabitants of the world will learn righteousness* (Isaiah 26:9). To "watch and pray" is Jesus' invitation to know Him and hold fast to His Word as we learn to stand with Him in the face of the head-winds before us.

As a general overview, it is vital to understand the biblical foundations for the import and relevancy of the "watchmen" as a movement today in preparing the Church for the future return of the Lord.

OVERVIEW:

Today, there is a distinctive call to "watch" as end-time prophetic events emerge on the global scene. A dynamic shift is taking place where personal prayer lives and intercession are shifting into a call to "watch." As we will see, the term "watch" is not simply praying, worshiping and declaring, but requires engagement with what we see happening in the world. As compared to one-on-one intercession, watchmen diligently search the horizon for the concerns of God, seek to understand His will, declare it, and act. A distinctive concern for watchmen is the moral and ethical condition of society. The Church today is being called to be a beacon of light in ever-increasing darkness as Jesus exhorted, *Let your light so shine before men, that they may see your good works and glorify your Father in heaven* (Matthew. 5:16).

Isaiah prophesied the relentless call of the watchmen: *I have set watchmen on your walls, O Jerusalem; they shall never hold their peace day or night. You who make mention of the Lord, do not keep silent, and give Him no rest till He establishes and till He makes Jerusalem a praise in the earth* (Isaiah 62:6-7). Interestingly, these very words were spoken in Jewish synagogues around the world on 9/11/2001. God was prophesying His answer while the catastrophic attacks were being executed. The attacks opened a significant gate of lawlessness and terror upon the earth—a true birth pang.

As we face the battles ahead, we need all hands on deck! As the end-time harvest looms and deposits of God's glory emerge in pockets throughout the earth, we need to foster greater collaboration and Kingdom advance amongst believers. William NeSmith, addresses these differences well:

> "It must be noted that each of us has a unique personality and there are many ways to engage with varying depth or extent for this involvement. Some are aggressive, some timid. Some are confident, some need encouragement. Some are contemplative, some are unreflective in their decision-making process. Some pray, some speak, some are hands on, some volunteer willingly, some need to be asked. Some are comfortable being out front while others prefer being out of the spotlight. Some take charge some prefer to be led. With regard to social resolution, some tend to focus on the benefits of prayer and intercession whereas some will pray less and act more."[2]

When we realize that each is called according to God's divine nature and plan, judgment towards one another ceases. Those who stand and are called to mobilize and contend for God's divine intervention have a positioning from God as valid as those pastoring churches or working on the streets, in schools, businesses, hospitals and courtrooms. Paul counsels and encourages us in 1 Corinthians 4:1-5:

> *Let a man so consider us, as servants of Christ and stewards of the mysteries of God. Moreover, it is required in stewards that one be found faithful. But with me it is a very small thing that I should be judged by you or by a human court. In fact, I do not even judge myself. For I know of nothing against myself, yet I am not justified by this; but He who judges me is the Lord.* **Therefore judge nothing before the time,** *until the Lord comes, who will both bring to light the hidden things of darkness and reveal the counsels of the hearts. Then each one's praise will come from God.*

Apprehending the visionary purpose and function of the watchman and its relevancy for believers today will become increasingly vital as times intensify. The routines of our past, our comfort zones of relating and contending, are of necessity shifting into the greater intentionality of the watchman. From Genesis to Revelation, the role of Watchman is interwoven throughout God's unfolding plans and purposes. There are three distinct biblical mandates in the role of the watchman: the individual call, community call, and the end-time call.

THE INDIVIDUAL CALL:

In times when deception works to lure our attention away from the foundations of Truth in the Scriptures, the origin of the term "watch" is vital to understand. It goes back to the creation of man in Genesis 2:15. The best description and foundational call for a "watchman" comes right from the Word itself. In the beginning God said, *"Let us make man in*

Our image, according to Our likeness" (Genesis 1:26). Genesis 2:15 further describes man's purpose, *Then the Lord God took the man and put him in the garden of Eden to tend and keep it.* "Tend" is the Hebrew word "abad," meaning to serve, execute, or husbandman. The word "keep" is the Hebrew word "shamar," meaning guard/defend, preserve, or "watch." In other words, God's intended purpose for humanity is to "serve and watch or defend" the garden He has given us. God created us to have fellowship with Him. He enjoyed walking in the garden with His creation. We were created in His image, Genesis 1:27. We are *all* called to be watchmen! Failure to do so has led to many of the destructive forces we now face on earth.

Today, many distractions and adversities captivate the hearts of men and women making us increasingly susceptible to deceptive schemes and secular narratives. As such, God is looking for those who will take the stance as "watchmen." He is looking for those who will guard and protect His Word and purpose—those who will—*Stand my watch and set myself on the rampart, and watch to see what He will say to me, and what I will answer when I am corrected* (Habakkuk 2:1).

Reviewing Jesus' teaching to the disciples of the end-times in Matthew 24-26, the word "watch" appears multiple times as both a warning and mandate. The Greek word for "watch," grēgoreuō; means keeping awake, i.e., watching, or giving diligent attention. Jesus' incitement to "watch" to His disciples highlights the importance of this function as His life physically on earth would soon be taken away. Consider His last exhortation to them in the Garden of Gethsemane, *"What! Could you not watch with Me one hour? Watch and pray, lest you enter into temptation. The spirit indeed is willing but the flesh is weak"* (Matthew 26:40b-41). These words to "watch and pray!" are equally important—and, I believe, aimed at us—today. Why? Because He knew our spirits would be willing, but our flesh is weak.

Jesus use of *watch* indicates a distinct function that feeds our *prayer*. Both are necessary as times intensify. It brings the horizontal view into our vertical relationship with God.

The role and function of the watchman bears the responsibility of caring for and defending God's laws, plans and purposes in our lives! Who God is, and how He moves to keep us aligned, centers around His New Covenant promises. Ruth Barton remarks, "Making and keeping covenants is the way God does relationships."[3] Watchmen are being called to contend for these promises and as a result have a special relationship and trust with God.

The culture around us can easily distract and incite us to move in our own direction, even with good intentions, unaware of the purposes of God. When the world makes it easy for us to exit commitments and relationships, God's plans can often be avoided rather than taking the high and challenging road to stand, persevere and build with one another.

The comfort in honoring covenant is that God never leaves us or forsakes us. He is a covenant keeping God. It is vital for us individually and corporately to have this sense of covenant or ownership—to wait on Him for His answers. When His plans are in place, if we stand for His covenant purposes—even at substantial cost. He will win, and we will be strengthened and trusted for more. "Shamar" and "grēgoreuō" are powerful words of God's call to mankind to protect His purposes for life in the face of increasing opposition and deception.

THE COMMUNITY CALL:

Though we are all called to be "watchmen," this mandate is being ushered forth to those who will receive and carry it. God is now preparing a company that has received the vision; and understands the importance of connecting as a community and who will work to collaborate across their cities, regions and nations intentionally. They will know each other and relate as an ekklesia.

Dean Briggs states, "The ekklesia are many voices, many perspectives, many prayers, conducted by the Spirit of Christ, blended into a governmental sound that commands the earth into alignment with

His will."[4] The very nature of the "watchman" requires a connection to a greater whole, i.e., community. Watchmen do not function in isolation. As such, community is a distinct characteristic that is shifting the prayer movement out of our individual stance and ministries into a watchmen movement. Being uniquely positioned, watchmen relate to one another, sound the rallying cry if necessary and mobilize accordingly.

Community and **committed corporate** prayer are foundational ingredients biblically and historically for the Church to fulfill its missional and Kingdom mandate "to make disciples of all nations" (Matthew 28:19). Such steadfastness carries the body of Christ full circle back to the ekklesia, the ruling governmental Church spoken of by Jesus in Matthew 16:18, *"And I tell you, you are Peter, and on this rock I will build my church, (ekklēsia[5]), and the gates of hell shall not prevail against it."* Briggs relays the importance of understanding such a community in prayer: "Very simply, ekklesia must be a 1) community 2) of prayer 3) in holiness and love or it cannot be an ekklesia. It is not peopled with lone rangers who demand heaven's enforcement of their carnal whims."[6]

Building community in prayer is a functional role of the watchman. Acts 2:1 and the story of Pentecost is a case where believers meeting in intense and committed corporate prayer birthed the New Testament church. The relational strength fostered in the corporate prayer community is not what we typically experience in a Sunday morning service. When people meet together for prayer, a close-knit kinship can develop between friends, as is seen in 2 Samuel 18:24-28. During the uprising of Absalom, the watchman was positioned between two gates and seated with David. Both were looking into the distance. The watchman first saw a runner and announced to David, *I think the running of the first is like the running of Ahimaaz the son of Zadok* (2 Sam. 18:27). How could he identify this person so accurately? He knew Ahimaaz well enough to know his gait, and that he would be carrying an important message. Today, God seeks those who will build communities of prayer from local expressions to global connections with the intentionality of relationship. Eventually, it will yield a day and night process that harnesses the resources of heaven to usher in the harvest.

One of the most significant revivals in history occurred in Herrnhut, Germany among what came to be known as the *Moravians* in the early 1700s. Under the leadership of Count Nicholas von Zinzendorf, a deeply divided community consisting of various refugee cultures from Europe, decided to live and work more in community and relationship. Subsequently, they developed a corporate prayer environment and committed to it.

On August 13, 1727, the Spirit of the Lord fell, igniting a 24/7 prayer and missions movement lasting well over 100 years. The *prayer and mission* dynamics expressed through these Moravians helped to launch the modern-day mission's movement. All continents on earth were impacted by the missionaries sent from this village. Herrnhut means "The Watch of the Lord."

Today, building a "Watchman" culture through relational strength will ideally lay the foundations of trust that inspire healthy, vibrant community life and committed prayer to strengthen any church, House of Prayer ministry or corporate expression. The Global Watch has a set of core values to facilitate sustained, healthy corporate prayer/worship environments.[7]

The pursuit of relational strength is a vital part of the "Watchman" function. As such, it is different than our personal intercessory stance. As it was in David's time and in biblical history, when the functions of a watchman are in place, they will yield health and vitality to any corporate expression, community or church. Such a posture carries a protective attribute and a redemptive call that speaks life into the community. Rather than interfere with corporate leadership structures, all engaged will be strengthened. As the leader of the Moravian revival, Count von Zinzendorf is noted as saying, "There can be no Christianity without community."[8]

THE END-TIME CALL:

Today, there is a global preparation as the end-time biblical narratives unfold before our eyes. The Church is being called out of complacency into the "watchful," awakened and alert Bride. COVID-19 has served to rattle the comfort zones of the church's four walls and incited new ways of "doing church." Unique to this calling is a desire to connect and build communities of committed prayer with a steady eye on the horizon and a concern for the times. Today, watchmen active in their local churches, businesses, houses of prayer, and prayer groups are establishing these contending communities, potentially impacting every cultural sphere. They are being called out of isolation with a desire to connect and build relationally across cities, states and nations. Many have been through intense warfare. If you are such a person, be of good courage! God has allowed it to train us to be relentless for such a time as this.

As Isaiah 62:6 prophesies, watchmen will be on the walls of Jerusalem and will not keep silent day or night until "Jerusalem is a praise in the earth." Isaiah prophesies, watchmen will be vital in establishing the centration of His Government as they relentlessly pray for the purposes and prophetic fulfillment of Jerusalem. They will be heralded forth from the nations as Isaiah 60:10 prophesies, "The sons of foreigners shall build up your walls." These walls are both physical and spiritual and paint the picture of the millennial city, the center of God's Government.

Those in Jerusalem, Israeli intercessors, may hold the physical walls as "priests of the Lord" (Isaiah 61:6). Isaiah, the prophetic wall-builder, prophesied a dynamic interaction will happen between the watchmen in the nations and the priests in the physical location of Jerusalem: *Strangers shall stand and feed your flocks, and the sons of the foreigner shall be your plowmen and your vinedressers.... You shall eat the riches of the Gentiles, and in their glory you shall boast* (Isaiah 61:5, 6b).

The spiritual walls of Jerusalem will be raised throughout the nations. These spiritual "Prayer" walls are spoken of prophetically in scriptures:

- *So I sought for a man among them who would make a wall, and stand in the gap before Me on behalf of the land, that I should not destroy it* (Ezekiel 22:30).
- *Woe to the foolish prophets...You have not gone up into the gaps to build a wall for the house of Israel to stand in battle on the day of the Lord* (Ezekiel 13:3-5).

The gaps in the wall are spiritual. God is calling watchmen to fill, stand in the gap between heaven and earth, watch, and declare His purposes to a world in need. Today, the headwinds and adversities hitting the nations are intense. Those building the prayer ramparts will need to be connected and will require greater intentionality in community and communication to meet the challenges ahead.

When Nehemiah rebuilt the walls of Jerusalem, the diaspora of Israelites returning to Jerusalem worked together through relationships and created an effective communication system. Families were set into position. A corporate strategy was created to help guard, defend, and keep their work as they were positioned. Nehemiah states, *Then I said to the nobles, the rulers, and the rest of the people, "The work is great and extensive, and we are separated far from one another on the wall. Wherever you hear the sound of the trumpet, rally to us there. Our God will fight for us"* (Nehemiah 4:19-20). Additionally, these families were given tools to build and weapons to defend themselves, v. 13. Of note, as the families worked together, none of them lost their identity, but rather they were strengthened!

So it is today—Watchmen are being called to build their ramparts locally and connect globally with Israel. Today, families represent churches, ministries, prayer groups, and houses of prayer committed to community and corporate prayer. They also represent the ramparts Habakkuk speaks of: *I will stand my watch and set myself on the **rampart,** and watch to see what He will say to me, and what I will*

161

answer when I am corrected (Habakkuk 2:1). Scriptures prophetically declare this end-time mandate for relational strength and communication. Watchmen across the nations will see "eye to eye" when Jesus returns. In other words, they will know one another and agree. We are now in the preparation stages for this unifying force to emerge. An emerging reality of Isaiah 52:8-10 is being set into motion:

> *Your watchmen shall lift up their voices, with their voices they shall sing together;* **For they shall see eye to eye when** *the Lord brings back Zion. Break forth into joy, sing together, You waste places of Jerusalem for the Lord has comforted His people, He has redeemed Jerusalem. The Lord has made bare His holy arm in the eyes of all the nations; and all the ends of the earth shall see the salvation of our God* (Isaiah 52:8-10) (see also Ezekiel 1:20-28) (Emphasis added.)

It is not only the call of the watchmen in this hour that will mobilize people into this role, making the study of the biblical end-time narrative crucial. Such study unveils a dimension and depth of Jesus's redemptive nature that can otherwise be glossed over. His pre-eminence, eternal love, and care for creation reach new levels of understanding as His redeeming nature is revealed in Scriptures from Genesis to Revelation. The End-Time Study Group at the International House of Prayer in Kansas City has identified one hundred and fifty chapters in the Bible that carry end-time messages.[9] Such studies grounded in the biblical narrative are critical. No matter your eschatology, as times intensify, knowing God has a powerful redemptive plan unfolding is a radical stimulus for faith. It is a priority in the Global Watch community to equip and train in the biblical end-time narrative. The times ahead are not going to get any easier.

As we equip ourselves in the end-time narrative, relationships build and ramparts connect, prayer walls worldwide will catalyze the emergence of the ready and alert Bride. They will be ready with oil in their lamps, wicks trimmed, and fire burning on the altar of their hearts waiting for the midnight cry: *Behold, the bridegroom is coming; go out to meet him!*

SUMMARY:

We are in a time when we must boldly shift our stance in the body of Christ. Complacent entrapments that have hedged us in must be exposed and re-envisioned and re-directed towards God's purposes. As He grips our hearts with the reality of His plans, a powerful preparation is underway for the "restoration of all things" (Acts 3:21).

Until the day of His coming, our hearts are on a journey. We are uniquely being prepared for the centrality of Jesus to manifest in our lives. There is a new level of intimacy, trust, faith and fear of the Lord to which He is calling us, His Church. A shift is happening. God is awakening hearts. As we respond to this awakening and pursue it, the Spirit will re-ignite us with fresh revelation. The Gospel of peace will spread to an increasingly distressed world.

This call of the watchmen will transpire across the timeline of God's end-time plan. Briggs states it well, "If we truly become governmentally organized around the mission of Christ, Satan knows his gates are doomed."[10] In other words, "the gates of hell" cannot prevail against the ready, awakened and watchful Bride. Those called into this movement will be part of the Bride—connected and communicating throughout the nations preparing for His return.

There is coming a day when a cry will be heard at midnight, *Behold the bridegroom is coming go out and meet him* (Matthew 25:6). The watchmen in the night will have oil in their lamps with wicks trimmed and ready for they have heeded the words, *Watch therefore, for you know neither the day nor the hour in which the Son of Man is coming* (Matthew 25:13). May it be unto you according to His Word!

DISCUSSION QUESTIONS:

1. How has your perspective of the biblical principle of the "Watchmen" expanded while reading these chapters?
2. What does it mean to you to "Watch and Pray?"
3. Discuss which of the Watchmen characteristics you would like to grow in:
   - The Individual Call
   - The Community Call
   - The End Time Call
4. What practical steps can you take to develop your personal prayer life? Community in prayer engagement? End-time discipleship?
5. What is the difference between a watchman and an intercessor?

PRAYER POINTS:

Pray for the growth of the revelation of the call to "Watch and Pray" in your community.

ACTION STEPS:

1. Watch and pray! Take steps to start or join a corporate prayer expression in your local church or region.
2. Take steps to equip yourself in the end-time biblical narrative. Theglobalwatch.com has resources and recommendations available.

And let us consider one another in order to
stir up love and good works,
Not forsaking the assembling of ourselves together,
As is the manner of some,
But exhorting one another, and so much the more
As you see the Day approaching.
Hebrews 10:24-25

Introduction

1. Strong's number #1577: ekklesia
2. Merriam Webster: "church" https://www.merriam-webster.com/dictionary/church
3. Thomas H. Troeger, *House of Prayer in the Heart: How homiletics nurtures the church's spirituality,* the article is a re-worked version of a presentation entitled, "The temple preaching builds: A house of prayer in the heart," originally given to the Festival of Homiletics in Spring of 2004 in Washington, DC.
4. John L. Whitsett, "Overcoming the Omission: A Study in determining the foundational beliefs and Values that Lead to Effective Implementation of Corporate Prayer in the North American Context." A PhD. Dissertation presented to the faculty of Asbury Theological Seminary," May 2013, Pg 26.
5. "List of Christian Movements," *Wikipedia*, https://en.wikipedia.org/wiki/List of Christian movements.
6. "About the International House of Prayer," https://www.ihopkc.org/about/.

Chapter 1: The Review: Biblical Foundations for the House of Prayer

1. Dean Briggs, *Ekklesia Rising: The authority of Christ in Communities of Contending Prayer* (Kansas City, MO: Champion Press, 2014).
2. John Stott, *The Message of Acts* (Downers Grove, IL; Intervarsity Press, 1990) Kindle edition, Location 74 of 8328.
3. Ibid.
4. Edward M. Bounds, *The Necessity of Prayer* (New York, NY: Fleming H. Revell Co., 1929), 140-141.
5 James Banks, The Lost Art of Praying Together (Grand Rapids, Mi.: Discovery House Publishers, 2009), 15.
6. P.J. Johnson, Operation World. "A Handbook for World Intercession" (Bromley, Kent, England: STL Publications, 1978), 15.
7. George Barna. "The Year's most Intriguing Findings, From Barna Research Studies," *Articles in Culture and Media,* December 17, 2001, https://www.barna.com/research/the-years-most-intriguing-findings-from-barna-research-studies/.

8. George Barna, "Five Years Later: 9/11 Attacks show no lasting influence on Americans' Faith." *Research Releases in Culture & Media,* August 28, 2006. https://www.barna.com/research/five-years-later-911-attacks-show-no-lasting-influence-on-americans-faith/.

9. Banks, *The Lost art of Praying Together,* 15.

10. John Spina, "Corporate Prayer in the Book of Acts: Lessons for the American Church," Masters Thesis. Reformed Theological Seminary, Western Illinois University, 1976, 6.

11. Howard Lawler, *The Corporate Prayer Challenge: 30 Days to Kickstart the Change We Need* (Wake Forest, NC; Salpizo Publications, 2020), pg. 16 Kindle Edition location 219 of 2229.

12. Tony Ridgaway, "Prayer Statistics: Statistics on Prayer in the U.S." *Church Leaders,* May 5, 2011/ Access July 30, 2021. https://churchleaders.com/pastors/pastor-articles/150915-u-s-statistics-on-prayer.html May 5.

13. George Barna, "Silent and Solo: Howe\ Americans Pray," Research Releases in Faith & Christianity, August 15, 2017 https://www.barna.com/research/silent-solo-americans-pray.

14. Jeanet Bentzen, "In Crisis, We Pray: Religiosity and COVID 19 Pandemic," CEPR Discussion Paper, DP14824, June 2020, https://www.economics.ku.dk/research/corona/Bentzen_religiosity_covid.pdf, 1.

15. John L. Whitsett, "Overcoming the omission; A Study in determining the foundational beliefs and Values that Lead to Effective Implementation of Corporate Prayer in the North American Context." Asbury Theological Seminary, May 2013. https://place.asburyseminary.edu/cgi/viewcontent.cgi?article=1730&context=ecommonsatsdissertations, 19.

16. Dr. Olusoga Martins Akintunde, "Modeling Prayer in Luke-Acts for Effective Church Growth in Changing Cultures," An Applied Research Project presented to the Faculty of the Department of Educational Ministries and Leadership, Dallas Theological Seminary, April, 2015, 7.

17. Stott, *The Message of Acts,* Location 74 of 8328.

18. Banks, *The Lost Art of Praying Together,* 44.

19. John Franklin, *And the Place was Shaken.* (Nashville, TN: Broadman & Holman Publishers, 2005), 10.

20. Ben Patterson, "Whatever happened to the Prayer Meeting?" *CT Pastors,* www.christianitytoday.com/pastors/1999/fall/9l4120.html, 3.

21. George Buttrick. *Prayer* (New York NY: Abingdon-Cokesbury Press, 1945), 271.

22. Ibid. Location 816 of 8328.

23. Dean Briggs. "The Seventh Greatest Spiritual Platform Shift in History," September 26, 2020/Access July, 2021. https://deanbriggs.com/the-seventh-greatest-spiritual-platform-shift-in-history/.

_____

24. Lawler, *The Corporate Prayer Challenge,* pg 141, Location 1900 of 2229.

Chapter 2: The Review: The Character and Nature of Corporate Prayer in the Early Church and Book of Acts

1. Stott, *The Message of Acts*, Location 60 of 8328.
2. Akintunde, "Modeling Prayer in Luke-Acts for Effective Church Growth in Changing Cultures," 7.
3. Spina, "Corporate Prayer in the Book of Acts," iii.
4. D. Edmond Hiebert, Working with God: Scriptural Studies in Intercession (BJU Press, Greenville, SC, 2003) p. 19-20.
5. Stott. *The Message of Acts,* Location 641 of 8328.
6. Polhill, *The New American Commentary: An Exegetical and Theological Exposition of Holy Scripture, Acts,* (Nashville, TN: Broadman Press, 2001), 85, Loc 2222 of 19561.
7. Strong's # g4342 ", προσκαρτερέω proskartereō;
8. Stott, *The Message of Acts,* location 850 of 8328.
9. Ibid.
10. Ibid., location 932 of 8328.
11. John Polhill, *The New American Commentary: An Exegetical and Theological Exposition of Holy Scripture, Acts,* 182.
12. Stott, *The Message of Acts*, location 1348-1433.
13. Polhill, *The New American Commentary,* 119.
14. "Acts 3," *Matthew Henry Commentary on the Whole Bible* on-line version, https://www.biblestudytools.com/commentaries/matthew-henry-complete/acts/3.html.
15. Polhill, *The New American Commentary*, pg 125.
16. Ibid. pg 164.
17. Strong's g3954; παρρησία parrēsia.
18. Stott, *The Message of Acts*, location 1686 of 8328.

Chapter 3: The Reason: Why Corporate Prayer? The Empowered Church

1. Dean Briggs, *Ekklesia Rising*, pg 214.
2. Stott, *The Message of Acts,* location 816 of 8328.
3. Polhill, *The New American Commentary:* pg151 of 548, Loc 3969 of 19561.

4. Armin Gesswein,. *With One Accord in One Place: The Role of Prayer in the Early Church* (Terre Haute, IN, Prayershop Publishing, 2014). Kindle Edition Location 195 of 1116.

5. Strong's g3661; ὁμοθυμαδόν homothymadon.

6. Ibid.

7. Polhill, *The New American Commentary* pg 121.

8. Spina, "Corporate Prayer in the Book of Acts," pg 27.

9. Stott, *The Message of Acts* Location 816 of 8328.

10. Ibid, pg 827 of 8328.

11. Whitsett, "Overcoming the Omission," pg 68.

12. J. Edwin Orr, "Prayer and Revival." https://finishingthetask.com/about-finishing-the-task/people-group-list/, pg 1.

13. Ibid.

14. Ibid.

15. George Peters, *A Biblical Theology of Missions*, Moody Publishers, January 1, 1984, pg 300.

16. Michael Cooper, "On Earth as it is in heaven: The Haystack Revival," December 17, 2007/ Access July 31, 2021. https://mcoopjr.blogspot.com/2007/12/haystack-revival.html.

17. Steve Hawthorne, "United, Focused Prayer: Changes in the Way We are Praying for the World, Part 1"; Lausanne World Pulse Archives, Issue: 12-2008. https://lausanneworldpulse.com/themedarticles-php/1063/12-2008.

18. Barna, "Silent and Solo: How Americans Pray" June 5-9, 2017.

19. "US News & Beliefnet Prayer Survey," https://www.beliefnet.com/faiths/faith-tools/meditation/2004/12/u-s-news-beliefnet-prayer-survey-results.aspx.

20. "The UPPG List," Finishing the Task. July 8, 2021/Access date: August, 2021, https://finishingthetask.com/about-finishing-the-task/people-group-list/

21. Francis Frangipane, *The three Battle-grounds*, (Marion, Iowa, River of Life Ministries, 1989), 15,21.

22. George Peters, *A Biblical Theology of Missions*, (Chicago, IL, Moody Publishers, 1984) 300.

23. Stott, *The Message of Acts,* Location 74 of 8328.

24. Gesswein, *With One Accord,* Location 459 of 1116.

25. Whitsett, "Overcoming the Omission," 19.

26. Stott, *The Message of Acts,* Location 1937 of 8328.

27. Rev. John Greenfield, "Power from on High: The Great Moravian Revival," The Gospel Truth. Access July 30, 2021. https://www.gospeltruth.net/moravian.htm .

28. Whitsett, "Overcoming the Omission," pg 40.

29. Talbot W. Chambers. *The New York City Noon Prayer Meeting: A Simple Prayer Gathering that Changed the World*, (Shippensburg, PA, Arsenal Press, 2019), 70.

Chapter 4: The Report: Present-Day Challenges

1. Jim Cymbala, *Fresh Wind Fresh Fire* (Grand Rapids, MI: Zondervan, 1997), 92.

2. Banks, *The Lost Art of Praying Together*, 12.

3. Barna, "Silent and Solo: The State of Prayer in the American Church,"

4. D. Edmond Hiebert, *Working with God through Prayer*, (Greenville, SC: Bob Jones University Press, 1991) 19-20.

5. Gesswein, *With One Accord,* Location 1003 of 1116.

6. John Spina, "Corporate Prayer in the Book of Acts," iii.

7. Barna, "Silent and Solo."

8. Ridgaway, "Prayer Statistics: Statistics on Prayer in the U.S."

9. Whitsett, *Overcoming the Omission,* 47.

10. The Association of Religion Data Archives. *"General Social Survey 2014 Cross-Section and Panel Combined"* http://www.thearda.com/QuickStats/QS_104.asp

11. Edmund P. Clowney. "A Biblical Theology of Prayer" in *Teach us to Pray: Prayer in the Bible and the World* (Eugene, OR: Wipf and Stock Publishers, 2002),   12.

12. Ibid.

13. Richard J. Foster. *Prayer: Finding the Heart's True Home* (San Francisco, CA: Harper, San Francisco, 1992).

14. Whitsett, "Overcoming the Omission," 47.

15. Ibid., 2.

16. Ibid., 17-18.

17. Patterson, "Whatever happened to the prayer meeting?" 2.

18. Whitsett, "Overcoming the Omission." 18.

19. "Secularization," https://en.wikipedia.org/wiki/Secularization.

20. Dr. EK Foshaugen, "The Role of religion in COVID 19 Pandemic, Considering Pippa Norris' and Ronald Inglehart's secularization theory, https://www.researchgate.net/profile/Edvard-Foshaugen/publication/343761312_The_role_of_religion_in_the_Covid19_pandemic_considering_Norris_and_Inglehart/links/5f3e4b64458515b729313ad8/The-role-of-religion-in-the-Covid19-pandemic-considering-Norris-and-In, 2.

21. Patterson, "Whatever happened to the prayer meeting?" 2.

22. Whitsett, "Overcoming the Omission," 4.

23. Edmund P. Clowney. "A Biblical Theology of Prayer" in *Teach us to Pray: Prayer in the Bible and the World*. (Eugene, OR: Wipf and Stock Publishers, 2002),   143.

24. Strong's h1847 *da'at*.

25. Jeff A. Benner, "Wisdom, Knowledge and Understanding." Ancient Hebrew Research Center. Accessed August 22, 2021. https://www.ancient-hebrew.org/studies-words/wisdom-knowledge-and-understanding.htm

26. Ibid.

27 . Ibid.

28. Strong's h3045 *yâḏa*.

29. Oliver W. Price. *"The Power of Praying Together."* (Grand Rapids: Kregel Pub, 1999) 15.

30. Banks, *The Lost Art of Praying Together,* 15.

31. Aiden Wilson, "Tozer Quotes about Revival," AZ Quotes, Accessed July 30, 2021, https://www.azquotes.com/quote/550383.

32. Jeanet Bentzen, "In Crisis, We Pray: Religiosity and the COVID-19 Pandemic," University of Copenhagen, Abstract. https://www.economics.ku.dk/research/corona/ Bentzen_religiosity_covid.pdf.

33. Whitsett, pg 72.

34. George Barna, "Most Christians View Their Faith as a Force for Good," *Articles in Faith & Christianity*, March 16, 2016. https://www.barna.com/research/most-christians-view-their-faith-as-a-force-for-good/. Accessed Nov. 19, 2019.

35. Katayoun Kishi "Christians faced widespread harassment in 2015, but mostly in Christian-majority countries." Pew Research, https://www.pewresearch.org/fact-tank/2017/06/09/christians-faced-widespread-harassment-in-2015-but-mostly-in-christian-majority-countries/ June 9, 2017.

36. Samirah Majumdar, "Government restrictions on religion around the world reached a new record in 2018," Pew Research, November 10, 2020/Access July, 2021; https://www.pewresearch.org/fact-tank/2020/11/10/government-restrictions-on-religion-around-the-world-reached-new-record-in-2018/.

37. Ibid.

38. Ibid.

39. Lewis Thompson, *How to Conduct Prayer Meetings, or an Account of Some Meetings.*
That Have Been Held. (Boston, MA: D. Lothrop and Co., 1880), pg.17.

40. Ibid., 68.

Chapter 5: The Reset: Lessons from the Seven Churches of Revelation

1. Akintunde, "Modeling Prayer in Luke," pg 5.

2. Ibid.

3. Cheryl Sacks, Cheryl Sacks, *The Prayer Saturated Church: A Comprehensive Handbook for Prayer Leaders* (Colorado Springs, CO: Navpress, 2007), 29.

4. George Barna, "A New generation of Pastors Places its Stamp on Ministry," *Research Releases in Leaders & Pastors,* February 17, 2004/ Accessed July 31, 2021,

https://www.barna.com/research/a-new-generation-of-pastors-places-its-stamp-on-ministry/.

5. Sacks, *The Prayer Saturated Church,* 177.

6. Jim Haesemeyer, "The Church of Laodicea: the Church that Grew Too Comfortable," August 10, 2019/ Accessed June 20, 2021, https://renewinknowledge.org/study-on-the-church-of-laodicea/.

7. Adam W. Greenway, "Restoring the church's first love: a case study from the church at Ephesus," Southern Seminary Magazine, Summer 2014/ Access July 30, 2021, https://equip.sbts.edu/article/church-revitalization-restoring-the-churchs-first-love/.

8. Tom Lowe, "Commentary on the Book of Revelation," April 30, 2015/ Access July 15, 2021, https://godisstillgood.wixsite.com/revelation-of-john/the-church-at-smyrna-.

9. The Martyrdom of Polycarp, "#103: Polycarp's Martyrdom." Cristian History Institute. Edited and prepared for the web by Dan Graves. Access August 9, 2021, https://christianhistoryinstitute.org/study/module/polycarp/.

10. Nilay Saiya, Stuti Manchanda, "Paradoxes of Pluralism, Privilege, and Persecution: Explaining Christian Growth and Decline Worldwide," Sociology of Religion, April 7, 2021, https://academic.oup.com/socrel/advance-article-abstract/doi/10.1093/socrel/srab006/6213975.

11. Ibid.

12. Steve Sewell, "Commentary on the Book of Revelation – (2:12-17)-Pergamum," Theology First, https://theologyfirst.org/commentary-on-revelation-212-17pergamum

13. The Salt of the Earth, "The Doctrine and Works of the Nicolaitans, April 9, 2019, https://www.the-saltoftheearth.com/nicolaitans/.

14. Strongs g5281, hypomonē.

15. Steve Sewell, "Commentary on Revelation, Thyatira" Theology First, November 9, 2019/Accessed July 15, 2021, https://theologyfirst.org/commentary-on-revelation-218-29-thyatira/.

16. Steve Sewell, "Commentary on Revelation, Sardis," Theology First, November 12, 2019/ Accessed July 15, 2021, https://theologyfirst.org/commentary-on-revelation-31-6-sardis/, November 12, 2019.

17. Ibid.

18. Paul Luckraft, "The Letter to Sardis," Prophecy Today: Teaching Articles, January 20, 2017/Access August 9, 2021, https://prophecytoday.uk/study/teaching-articles/item/595-the-letter-to-sardis.html.

19. Strongs g1127, grēgoreuō.

20. Steve Sewell, "Commentary on Revelation 3:7-13," Theology First, November 15, 2019/Accessed July 15, 2021, https://theologyfirst.org/commentary-on-revelation-37-13-philidelphia/.

21. Sewell, "Commentary on Revelation 3:14-22, The Church at Laodicea," Theology First, November 15, 2019/ Accessed July 15, 2021, https://theologyfirst.org/commentary-on-revelation-314-22-laodicea/.

Chapter 6: The Revitalization: Stepping Forward in Faith

1. Stott, *The Message of Acts*, loc 1418 of 8328.

2. Jeff Banks, *The Lost Art of Praying Together,* 19.

3. "The History of IHOPKC" https://www.ihopkc.org/prophetichistory/

4. "IHOPKC History" https://www.ihopkc.org/about/.

5. 24-7prayer.com. *It all Started by Accident* https://www.247prayer.com/story#/24-7story/prayer-explosion.

6. 24-7 Prayer Ministry Directory. http://www.24-7prayerlist.com/index.html,

7. "US News & Beliefnet Prayer Survey Results," *Beliefnet,* accessed July 15, 2021. https://www.beliefnet.com/faiths/faith-tools/meditation/2004/12/u-s-news-beliefnet-prayer-survey-results.aspx.

8. Ronald Heifetz, Marty Linsky, *Leadership on the Line* (Boston, MA: Harvard Business School Publishing, 2002), 63.

9. Ibid., 51.

10. Lea, Larry, *Could You Not Tarry: Learning the Joy of Prayer* (Lake Mary, FL: Charisma House), 5-6.

11. Henry Nouwen, *The Return of the Prodigal Son Anniversary Edition*. (New York: Image Books, 1992), Kindle location 629 of 4201.

12. Peter Grieg, David Blackwell, *The 24-7 Prayer Manual,* (Ontario, Canada: David C. Cook, 2008), Kindle Location 529 of 1400.

13. Ruth Barton, *Pursuing God Together* (Downer's Grove, IL: Intervarsity Press, 2012), 56.

14. Strong's h1556, gâlal.

15. Lawler, *The Corporate Prayer Challenge,* 139 of 163, Location 1864 of 2229.

16. Arthur Boers. *Servants and Fools: A Biblical Theology of Leadership* (Nashville, TN: Abingdon Press, 2015) 104; Location 2570 of 4791.

17. Ibid. 96; Location 2401 of 4791.

18 John Maxwell, *The 17 Indisputable laws of Teamwork*. (Nashville, TN: Thomas Nelson, 2001) 21.

19. Ed Silvoso, *Ekklesia,* (Bloomington, MN: Chosen Books, 2017) 234.

20. Roger Heuser, *Leading the Congregation: Caring for Yourself while Serving the People*, (Nashville, TN, Abingdon Press, 2010) Kindle locations 1588-1589.

21. Robert Quinn. *Deep Change* (San Francisco, CA: Jossey-Bass Publishers, 1996), 128.

22. Ibid., 53.

Chapter 7: The Re-engagement: Prayer and Action

1. Stephanie Hertzenberg, "3 Times Prayer Changed History," Beliefnet.com. https://www.beliefnet.com/inspiration/3-times-prayer-changed-history.aspx

2. Banks, *The Lost Art of Praying Together,* 69.

3. Robert Mulholland, Invitation to a Journey: A Road Map for Spiritual Formation (Downer's Grove, IL: InterVarsity Press, 1993), 141.

4. Strong's h3533, k̲âb̲aš;

5. Bill Nesmith.. *Christians & Politics: A Biblical Response: The Bridegroom is Coming: It is Time to Get "Engaged"* (Windham, CT: Harvest Light, 2020). Kindle Edition. 1098 3187.

6. Hertzenberg, "3 Times Prayer Changed History."

7. Ibid.

8. David Barton, *The American Story: The Beginnings* (Aledo, TX: Wallbuilders, 2020), 92-95.

9. Ibid., 110-111.

10. Samuel Smith, "Calif. Prosecutor threatens church with closure, jail sentences for COVID-19 order violation," Christian Post 8/20/20, Accessed September 2021, https://www.christianpost.com/news/calif-prosecutor-threatens-church-with-closure-jail-sentences-for-covid-19-order-violation.html

11. Carly Mayberry, "Pasadena's Harvest Church Wins Lawsuit Against Gavin Newsom, Lifting Worship Restrictions" Newsweek 5/20/21, Accessed September 2021, https://www.newsweek.com/pasadenas-harvest-church-wins-lawsuit-against-gavin-newsom-lifting-worship-restrictions-1593096#:~:text=On%20Monday%2C%20a%20California%20District%20Court%20entered%20an,impose%20discriminatory%20restrictions%20upon%20any%20houses%20of%20worship.

12. Os Hillman, "The 7 Cultural Spheres – Being Salt and Light in Key Areas of Society," August 1, 2019, Accessed September, 2021, https://godtv.com/the-7-cultural-spheres/.

Chapter 8: The Redeemed: God is Love

1. Strong's h1980 hâlak̲.

2. Russell Moore, "The Spirit of Adoption (Exposition of Romans 8:12-17)," https://pastorhistorian.com/2009/08/02/the-spirit-of-adoption-exposition-of-romans-812-17/

3. A.W. Tozer, *The Knowledge of the* Holy (New York: Harper Collins, 1961), pg 7.
4. Heuser, *Leading the Congregation,* Kindle locations 1523-1524.
5. Heifetz, *Leadership on the Line,* pg195.
6. Curt Thompson, MD, *Anatomy of the Soul* (Carol Stream, IL: Tyndale House Publishers, 2010), 172.
7. Ibid. 180.
8. Wei Deng, James B. Aimone, Fred H Gage, "New neurons and new memories: how does adult hippocampal neurogenesis affect learning and memory?" Nat Rev Neuroscience, May 2010; 11(5):339. https://pubmed.ncbi.nlm.nih.gov/20354534/.
9. Quinn, *Deep Change,* 45.
10. Heuser, *Leading the Congregation*, location 1555 of 6820.
11. Sherwood Lingenfelter, *Leading Cross-Culturally* (Grand Rapids MI: Baker Academic, 2008), 19.

Chapter 9: The Reform: Prepare the Way

1. Larry Lea, *Could You Not Tarry One Hour?* Lake Mary, FL: Charisma House Book Group, 1987

Chapter 10: The Return: Watch and Pray

1. Strong's g1127 grēgoreuō
2. Bill NeSmith, *Christians & Politics: A Biblical Response: The Bridegroom is Coming: It is Time to Get "Engaged"* (Windham, CT: Harvest Light, 2020) (Kindle Edition) Location 1009 of 3187
3. Barton, *The American Story,* pg 155.
4. Briggs, *Ekklesia,* pg 189.
5. Strong's g1577 ekklēsia.
6 .Briggs, *Ekklesia,* pg 187.
7. "Core Values and Beliefs," **https://www.theglobalwatch.com/core-values-and-beliefs.html**
8. **http://img.sermonindex.net/modules/articles/article_pdf.php?aid=32366.**
9. Center for Biblical End-time Studies, https://www.ihopkc.org/cbets/
10. Briggs, *Ekklesia,* 208.

BIBLIOGRAPHY

1. Akintunde, Dr. Olusoga Martins Akintunde. "Modeling Prayer in Luke-Acts fpr Effective Church Growth in Changing Cultures." An Applied Research Project presented to the Faculty of the Department of Educational Ministries and Leadership, Dallas Theological Seminary. April, 2015.

2. Banks, James. *The Lost Art of Praying Together.* (Grand Rapids, MI: Discovery, 2009).

3. Barna, George. "The Year's most Intriguing Findings, From Barna Research Studies," *Articles in Culture and Media,* December 17, 2001, https://www.barna.com/research/the-years-most-intriguing-findings-from-barna-research-studies/.

4. Barna, George. "A New generation of Pastors Places its Stamp on Ministry," *Research Releases in Leaders & Pastors,* February 17, 2004/Access date July 30, 2021, https://www.barna.com/research/a-new-generation-of-pastors-places-its-stamp-on-ministry/.

5. Barna, George. "Five Years Later: 9/11 Attacks show no lasting influence on Americans' Faith." *Research Releases in Culture & Media,* August 28, 2006/ Access date July 29, 2021, https://www.barna.com/research/five-years-later-911-attacks-show-no-lasting-influence-on-americans-faith/.

6. Barna, George. "Most Christians View Their Faith as a Force for Good," *Articles in Faith & Christianity*, March 16, 2016/ Access date July 30, 2021, https://www.barna.com/research/most-christians-view-their-faith-as-a-force-for-good/.

7. Barna, George. "Silent and Solo: Howe\ Americans Pray," *Research Releases in Faith & Christianity*, August 15, 2017/Access date July 30, 2021, https://www.barna.com/research/silent-solo-americans-pray.

8. Barna, George. "Trends: What's New and What's Next," December, 2016/ Access date July 30, 2021, https://www.barna.com/research/barna-trends-whats-new-whats-next/

9. Barton, Ruth Haley. *Pursuing God's Will Together*. Downer's Grove, IL: Intervarsity Press, 2012.

10. Benner, Jeff A. "Wisdom, Knowledge and Understanding." Ancient Hebrew Research Center. Accessed August 22, 2021, https://www.ancient-hebrew.org/studies-words/wisdom-knowledge-and-understanding.htm

11. Bentzen, Jeanet. "In Crisis, We Pray: Religiosity and COVID 19 Pandemic," CEPR Discussion Paper, DP14824, June 2020.

12. Boers, Arthur. *Servants and Fools: A Biblical Theology of Leadership*. Nashville, TN: Abingdon Press, 2015.

13. Bounds, Edward M. *The Necessity of Prayer*. New York, NY: Fleming H. Revell Co., 1929.

14. Briggs, Dean. *Ekklesia Rising*. Champion Press, Kansas City, MO, 2014.

15. Briggs, Dean. "The Seventh Greatest Spiritual Platform Shift in History," September 26, 2020/Access July 30, 2021. https://deanbriggs.com/the-seventh-greatest-spiritual-platform-shift-in-history/

16. Buttrick, George. *Prayer*. New York NY: Abingdon-Cokesbury Press, 1945.

17. Campolo, Tony. *Let Me Tell You a Story.* Nashville, TN: Thomas Nelson, 2000.

18. Chambers, Talbot W. *The New York City Noon Prayer Meeting: A Simple Prayer Gathering that Changed the World.* Shippensburg, PA: Arsenal Press, 2019.

19. Clowney, Edmund. *"A Biblical Theology of Prayer"* in *Teach us to Pray: Prayer in the Bible and the World.* Eugene, OR: Wipf and Stock Publishers, 2002.

20. Cooper, Michael. "On Earth as It Is in Heaven: The Haystack Revival," 17 Dec. 2007, mcoopjr.blogspot.com/2007/12/haystack-revival.html.

21. Cymbala, Jim. *Fresh Wind, Fresh Fire.* Grand Rapids, MI: Zondervan, 1994.

22. Espinoza, Chip; Ukleja,Mick. *Managing the Millennials: Discover the Core Competencies for Managing Today's Workforce.* Hoboken, NJ: John Wiley & Sons, 2016.

23. Foshaugen, Dr. E.K. "The Role of Religion in COVID 19 Pandemic, Considering Pippa Norris' and Ronald Inglehart's secularization theory," Research Gate, May 2020/ Access July 30, 2021. https://www.researchgate.net/profile/Edvard-Foshaugen/publication/343761312_The_role_of_religion_in_the_Covid19_pandemic_considering_Norris_and_Inglehart/links/5f3e4b64458515b729313ad8/The-role-of-religion-in-the-Covid19-pandemic-considering-Norris-and-In

24. Foster, J. Richard. *Prayer: Finding the Heart's True Home.* San Francisco, CA: Harper Pub., 1992.

25. Frangipane, Francis. *The three Battle-grounds*. Marion, Iowa: River of Life Ministries, 1989.

26. Franklin, John. *And the Place Was Shaken*. Nashville, TN: Broadman & Holman Publishers, 2005.

27. Gesswein, Armin. *With One Accord in One Place: The Role of Prayer in the Early Church*. Terre Haute, IN: Prayershop Publishing, 2014. Kindle Edition.

28. Greenway, Adam. "Restoring the church's first love: a case study from the church at Ephesus." Southern Seminary Magazine. Summer 2014. https://equip.sbts.edu/article/church-revitalization-restoring-the-churchs-first-love/

29. Grieg, Peter; Blackwell,David. *The 24-7 Prayer Manual*. Ontario, Canada: David C. Cook, 2008.

30. Haesemeyer, Jim. "The Church of Laodicea: the Church that Grew Too Comfortable." August 10, 2019/ Access July 30, 2021. https://renewinknowledge.org/study-on-the-church-of-laodicea/

31. Hawthorne, Steve. "United, Focused Prayer: Changes in the Way We are Praying for the World, Part 1." Lausanne World Pulse Archives, Issue: 12-2008. https://lausanneworldpulse.com/themedarticles-php/1063/12-2008.

32. Heifetz Ronald; Linsky, Marty. *Leadership on the Line*. Boston, MA: Harvard Business School Publishing, 2002.

33. Henry, Matthew. "Acts 3, Matthew Henry Commentary on the Whole Bible on-line version," https://www.biblestudytools.com/commentaries/matthew-henry-complete/acts/3.html

34. Hertzenberg, Stephanie. "3 Times Prayer Changed History." https://www.beliefnet.com/inspiration/3-times-prayer-changed-history.aspx

35. Heuser, Roger. *Leading the Congregation: Caring for Yourself while Serving the People.* Nashville, TN, Abingdon Press, 2010. Kindle.

36. Hiebert, D. Edmond. *Working with God through Prayer.* Greenville, SC: Bob Jones University Press, 1991.

37. Johnson, PJ. *Operation World. A Handbook for World Intercession.* Bromley, Kent, England: STL Publications, 1978.

38. Kishi, Katayoun. "Christians faced widespread harassment in 2015, but mostly in Christian-majority countries." Pew Research. June 9, 2017/ Access July 30, 2021. https://www.pewresearch.org/fact-tank/2017/06/09/christians-faced-widespread-harassment-in-2015-but-mostly-in-christian-majority-countries/ .

39. Lawler, Howard. *The Corporate Prayer Challenge: 30 Days to Kickstart the Change We Need.* Wake Forest, NC: Salpizo Publications, 2020, Kindle Edition.

40. Lea, Larry. *Could You Not Tarry One Hour?* Lake Mary, FL: Charisma House Book Group, 1987.

41. Lingenfelter, Sherwood. *Leading Cross-Culturally.* Grand Rapids MI: Baker Academic, 2008.

42. Lowe, Tom, "Commentary on the Book of Revelation," November 12, 2019. https://godisstillgood.wixsite.com/revelation-of-john/the-church-at-smyrna-.

43. Luckraft, Paul. "The Letter to Sardis." Prophecy Today. January 20, 2017/Access August 9, 2021. https://prophecytoday.uk/study/teaching-articles/item/595-the-letter-to-sardis.html.

44. Majumdar, Samirah. "Government restrictions on religion around the world reached a new record in 2018," Pew Research, November 10, 2020/Access July 30, 2021. https://www.pewresearch.org/fact-tank/2020/11/10/government-restrictions-on-religion-around-the-world-reached-new-record-in-2018/

45. Maxwell, John. *The 17 Indisputable Laws of Leadership.* Nashville, TN: Thomas Nelson, Inc., 2001.

46. Mayberry, Carly. "Pasadena's Harvest Church Wins Lawsuit Against Gavin Newsom, Lifting Worship Restrictions" Newsweek 5/20/21, Accessed September 2021. https://www.newsweek.com/pasadenas-harvest-church-wins-lawsuit-against-gavin-newsom-lifting-worship-restrictions-1593096#:~:text=On%20Monday%2C%20a%20California%20District%20Court%20entered%20an,impose%20discriminatory%20restrictions%20upon%20any%20houses%20of%20worship.

47. Moore, Russell. *"The Spirit of Adoption (Exposition of Romans 8:12-17),"* August 2, 2009/Access July 15, 2021. https://pastorhistorian.com/2009/08/02/the-spirit-of-adoption-exposition-of-romans-812-17/

48. Mulholland, Robert Jr. *Invitation to a Journey: A Road Map for Spiritual Formation.* Downer's Grove, IL: InterVarsity Press, 1993.

49. NeSmith, William. *Christians & Politics: A Biblical Response: The Bridegroom is Coming: It is Time to Get "Engaged"* Windham, CT: Harvest Light, 2020. Kindle.

50. Nouwen, Henry J.M. *The Return of the Prodigal Son Anniversary Edition.* New York: Image Books, 1992. Kindle.

51. Orr, J. Edwin. "Prayer and Revival." Accessed August, 2021. https://finishingthetask.com/about-finishing-the-task/people-group-list/.

52. Patterson, Ben. "Whatever Happened to Prayer Meeting?" Christianity Today. Accessed July 29, 2021. www.christianitytoday.com/pastors/1999/fall/9l4120.html.

53. Peters, George. *A Biblical Theology of Missions.* Chicago, IL: Moody Publishers, 1984.

54. Polhill, John. *The New American Commentary: An Exegetical and Theological Exposition of Holy Scripture, Acts*, Vol. 26. Nashville, TN: Broadman and Holman Publishers, 2001. Kindle.

55. Price, Oliver W. *The Power of Praying Together.* Grand Rapids: Kregel Pub, 1999.

56. Quinn, Robert. *Deep Change.* San Francisco, CA: Jossey-Bass Publishers, 1996.

57. Ridgaway, Toni. "Prayer Statistics: Statistics on Prayer in the U.S." *Church Leaders,* May 5, 2011/ Access July 30, 2021. https://churchleaders.com/pastors/pastor-articles/150915-u-s-statistics-on-prayer.html May 5.

58. Sacks, Cheryl. *The Prayer Saturated Church: A Comprehensive Handbook for Prayer Leaders.* Colorado Springs, CO: Navpress, 2007.

59. Saiya, Nilay; Manchanda, Stuti, "Paradoxes of Pluralism, Privilege, and Persecution: Explaining Christian Growth and Decline Worldwide," Sociology of Religion, April 7, 2021. https://academic.oup.com/socrel/advance-article-abstract/doi/10.1093/socrel/srab006/6213975.

60. Sewell, Steve. "Commentary on Revelation, Sardis." Theology First, November 12, 2019. https://theologyfirst.org/commentary-on-revelation-31-6-sardis/,

61. Sewell, Steve. "Commentary on Revelation 3:7-13, Philadelphia," Theology First, November 15, 2019.

https://theologyfirst.org/commentary-on-revelation-37-13-philidelphia/.

62. Sewell, Steve. "Commentary on Revelation 3:14-22, The Church at Laodicea," Theology First, November 16, 2019.

63. Silvoso, Ed. *Ekklesia.* Bloomington, MN: Chosen Books, 2017.

64. Smith, Samuel. "Calif. Prosecutor threatens church with closure, jail sentences for COVID-19 order violation," Christian Post 8/20/20, Accessed September 2021 https://www.christianpost.com/news/calif-prosecutor-threatens-church-with-closure-jail-sentences-for-covid-19-order-violation.html

65. Spina, John. *"Corporate Prayer in the Book of Acts: Lessons for the American Church,"* Master's Thesis. Reformed Theological Seminary, Western Illinois University. 1976.

66. Stott, John. *The Message of Acts.* Downers Grove, IL; Intervarsity Press, 1990. Kindle.

67. Strong, James. *Strong's Expanded Concordance*, New King James version with Strong's numbers Olive Tree Bible App.

68. Thompson, Curt, MD. *Anatomy of the Soul.* Carol Stream, IL: Tyndale House Publishers, 2010.

69. Thompson, Lewis. *How to Conduct Prayer Meetings, or an Account of Some Meetings That Have Been Held.* Boston, MA: D. Lothrop and Co., 1880.

70. Tozer, A.W. *The Knowledge of the Holy.* New York: Harper Collins, 1961.

71. Troeger, Thomas. "House of Prayer in the Heart: How Homiletics Nurtures the Church's Spirituality," The article is a re-worked version of a presentation entitled, "The temple preaching builds: A

house of prayer in the heart," originally given to the Festival of Homiletics in Spring of 2004 in Washington, DC.

72. Verwer, George. "Whatever Happened to the Prayer Meeting?" Sermonindex.net, January 18, 2013/ Access July 30, 2021. https://www.sermonindex.net/modules/newbb/viewtopic.php?topic _id=48096&forum=34.

73. Whitsett, John L. "Overcoming the Omission; A Study in Determining the Foundational Beliefs and Values that Lead to Effective Implementation of Corporate Prayer in the North American Context." Asbury Theological Seminary, May 2013. https://place.asburyseminary.edu/cgi/viewcontent.cgi?article=1730 &context=ecommonsatsdissertations.

74. Wilson, Aiden. *Tozer Quotes about Revival,* AZ Quotes. Accessed July 30, 2021. https://www.azquotes.com/author/14750-Aiden_Wilson_Tozer/tag/revival.

DIRECT WEBSITE

1. IHOPKC: "Center for End-time Biblical Studies," https://www.cbetskc.org

2. IHOPKC *"History."* https://www.ihopkc.org/about/.

3. IHOPKC *"Prophetic History".* https://www.ihopkc.org/prophetichistory/.

4. Prayer Ministry Directory. http://www.24-7prayerlist.com/index.html.

5. The Association of Religion Data Archives. *"General Social Survey 2014 Cross-Section and Panel Combined"* http://www.thearda.com/QuickStats/QS_104.asp.

6. The Global Watch Core Values and Beliefs: https://www.theglobalwatch.com/core-values-and-beliefs.html.

7. The Salt of the Earth. "The Doctrine and Works of the Nicolaitans," April 9, 2019; https ://www.the-saltoftheearth.com/nicolaitans/.

8. "US News & Beliefnet Prayer Survey," https://www.beliefnet.com/faiths/faith-tools/meditation/2004/12/u-s-news-beliefnet-prayer-survey-results.aspx.

9. 24-7prayer.com. *It all Started by Accident.* https://www.24-7prayer.com/story#/24-7story/prayer-explosion.